beer
drinker's
toolkit

A Gelding Street Press book
An imprint of Rockpool Publishing Pty Ltd
PO Box 252
Summer Hill, NSW 2130
Australia

www.geldingstreetpress.com
Follow us! 🄾 geldingstreet_press

Published in 2023 by Rockpool Publishing

ISBN: 9780645207101

Design by Daniel Poole, Rockpool Publishing
Edited by Heather Millar
Illustrated by Ellie Grant
Acquisition editor: Luke West, Rockpool Publishing

A catalogue record for this
book is available from the
National Library of Australia

NATIONAL LIBRARY OF AUSTRALIA

Printed and bound in China
10 9 8 7 6 5 4 3 2 1

beer drinker's toolkit

EQUIP YOURSELF TO NAVIGATE THE WORLD OF BEER

Mick Wüst

ILLUSTRATED BY ELLIE GRANT

This book is dedicated to my father-in-law Stephen, my friends Stu, Milika, and Adam …

In fact, to anyone who's asked me a question about beer and enjoyed my response.

This is for you – the answers to the questions you never asked.

Contents

07 | SECTION ONE

History according to beer 09

Beer today 21

Ingredients 35

Brewers and the brewing process 53

61 | SECTION TWO

Beer styles 63

Ales vs lagers 67

Pale lagers 71

Amber lagers and dark lagers 79

Pale ales 85

IPAs 93

Brown ales, porters and stouts 101

Sours 109

Other European beers 115

123 | SECTION THREE

Fresh is best 125

Serving up your beer 133

Engaging all five senses 149

The right beer at the right time 177

197 | SECTION FOUR

Ask Mick 199

Acknowledgements 213

About the author 214

introduction

They say
a little
knowledge is
a dangerous
thing.

Prepare to be
dangerous.

This book is for anyone who wants to know beer a little better.

Wherever you're at in your beer journey, I'm here to help you out with this – to give you the tools you need to navigate the world of beer … without turning you into a tool yourself.

I'm not a brewer or a certified beer expert. I'm a writer who started writing about beer in 2015 because beer is the funnest drink in the world. And the more I learn about this wonderful drink, the more I fall in love with it. So whenever I learn interesting things about beer, I want to share them with whoever will listen. Spread the knowledge and spread the love.

Beer is fun, so I reckon learning about beer should be fun as well. That's why this book is more like having a chat in a pub than sitting through a lecture. This isn't university.

Welcome to Schoonerversity – where the subject is beer, the classroom is your local brewery or bar, and the textbook is the book in your hand. Except instead of being boring and full of jargon, this textbook describes carbon dioxide as 'yeast burps'. (I actually think 'yeast farts' is funnier, but I know that grosses some people out. So I try to hold in any flatulence jokes. Forgive me if one slips out.)

In this book you'll find a blend of important facts and useless trivia, all heavily seasoned with bad jokes and loud opinions. I expect one day I'll be the old guy sitting in the corner of the pub, spouting my theories at anyone who makes the mistake of walking near me.

'Calling a beer "imperial" when it's only 8% ABV is cheating!'

'The darker the head, the better the stout.'

'You can improve any beer by 20% if you have it with a side of hot chips.'

I'm glad brewers and beer judges and researchers and whoever else take beer so seriously and use their impressive brains to dig into the science that beer requires. It's how we got to this golden age of beer with awesome breweries around every corner – and it's only getting better. And I'm glad they use those same brains to write more comprehensive and technical books than this one.

But when all is said and done, if you're happy to have your beer with a side of BS, then you're in the right place.

The world of beer is bigger and better than it's ever been before, and anyone who thinks beer is just a fizzy, yellow drink is kidding themselves. Wine is often seen as the drink to explore and learn about, but there's more variety and versatility in the world of beer than there is in wine – and it's more accessible too.

Not only is there an abundance of excellent breweries sending their beers far and wide, but there's probably one not far from where you are right now, brewing and pouring and selling different kinds of beer all the time. You can read the descriptions of the various brews, try a tasting paddle of several styles, and take a tour of the brewery. You can hear from the brewer's mouth how they go about making that sparkling pilsner or that pungent IPA (that's India pale ale, if you're new to the beer game) – and then you can taste the beer yourself.

If you're just discovering the variety of beer available, you're in for a treat. I remember the first IPA I tried – the bitterness just about burnt a hole through my tongue. (IPAs can be an acquired taste.) I remember the first beer I had with over 10% ABV (alcohol by volume) – it was a Belgian strong ale with a pirate ship on the label and it hit me like a tot of strong rum. (In retrospect, the pirate ship should have tipped me off.) I remember my first German wheat beer, my first breakfast stout, my first whisky barrel-aged beer.

There's nothing wrong with grabbing a cold beer for a hit of refreshment and the relaxing sigh of alcohol, but it's not the only way to enjoy beer.

I once gave a friend's boyfriend a sip of my beer. He said, 'That's really nice. But I couldn't drink a carton of it.'

I said, 'It's a 9% ABV Baltic porter. You're definitely not supposed to drink a carton of it.'

More and more people are beginning to appreciate beer in a multi-faceted way – understanding the ingredients, learning about the brewing process, exploring the aromas and flavours and textures of different beer styles.

Beer is for everyone

It's for my brother who's been drinking lagers his whole life but is becoming more and more interested in trying beers made by local breweries – including some of the fruity or dark beers he never liked before.

It's for my father-in-law who thought he didn't love beer because he didn't like bitterness but has spent the last couple of years discovering an array of malty and sweet and fruity beers.

It's for my friend who has a PhD in quantum physics but geeks out even harder on beer. She's gone from beer blogging to beer journalism to becoming a Certified Cicerone to becoming a professional brewer – and she isn't slowing down.

It's for the self-proclaimed 'Beer Tragic' in my hometown who supports every brewery, attends every beer event, tries every innovative new beer … and always loves going back to an old favourite made by one of the mega-breweries.

It's for me, the guy who drinks all kinds of fancy and innovative beer styles now, but who used to mix cheap lager with Pepsi when he wanted it weaker and vodka when he wanted it stronger. (If there are any beer police reading this: I was a teenager at the

time, so the statute of limitations has passed on those heinous crimes.) If you hear me say just one thing, let it be this: don't let anyone tell you how you *should* drink beer. While I'm going to spend this whole book suggesting different ways you *can* appreciate beer ... there are no rules in this book that can't be broken. No one can tell you what beer you should or shouldn't drink, like certain styles or breweries are off limits. No one can tell you how you should or shouldn't drink beer, like if you don't use a certain glass, you're somehow doing the beer a disservice.

Drink what you like, how you like it. If you want to smash clean lagers while eating greasy pizza and watching movies about rogue FBI agents, I hope you have a wonderful evening. If you want to pair a mixed ferment saison with organic oysters and French noir films, you have yourself a *merveilleuse soirée*.

Beer is fun. Don't overcomplicate it. The beer world has its share of people who take it seriously and get deep into the finicky details, and that's a great thing. But you don't have to do that to enjoy drinking it. There's no secret handshake or password you must know before you can join the inner circle of beer lovers.

Beer is meant to be enjoyed. Don't let anyone take that away from you.

Right. That's enough preamble. Time to get into the good stuff. Use this book however you like. Don't worry about reading it from cover to cover if that's not fun for you; it's not a novel and there's no test at the end. Flick through it. Look up your questions. Learn what you need when you need it. (The hard cover also works quite well as a beer coaster.)

Let's get cracking.

section one

We often think of beer as a product that's always been there, the same way rocks and water have always been there. But just like the grizzled detective in a noir film, beer has a backstory. And knowing where beer comes from can help you appreciate it all the more.

History according to beer

Some people will tell you the best beer is the one in your hand right now. But how can we ignore the history of a drink that's been enjoyed by Egyptian pharaohs and German monks alike?

We don't know exactly how beer was invented – it may have been an accident with wet bread or porridge getting a bit funky. But at some point thousands of years ago, people started making it on purpose. For most of history beer has been safer to drink than many water sources, so beer was a staple in homes around the world.

This timeline doesn't capture the whole story of beer. For example, women have done most of the brewing through history but haven't received the credit they deserve in the history books.

These pages are more like the scattered notes of a time traveller hiccupping through the space-time continuum, stopping every now and then for a beer and finding it ever more difficult to avoid stepping on a bug and altering history forever.

(Note: please don't drink and time travel.)

Timeline

3000 BC and earlier – Evidence of people brewing beer with different grains in Israel ~13000 BC, China ~7000 BC and Iran ~3000 BC (dates based on archaeological chemical evidence).

2500 BC – Workers building the Great Pyramids in Egypt get a ration of 4–5 litres of beer a day. But beer isn't just for the labourers – even the god-king pharaohs drink beer.

2200 BC – Babylonian king Hammurabi includes laws about beer pricing in the Code of Hammurabi.

1800 BC – Sumerian tablet records the *Hymn to Ninkasi*, the goddess of beer, which includes a recipe for how to brew beer.

1500–600 BC – Sura, a beer-like drink made from rice, is mentioned in Hindu texts the *Vedas* (1500–900 BC) and the *Ramayana* (600 BC).

400 BC – Evidence of people brewing beer with barley and oats in Britain.

332 BC–395 AD – Despite conquering a number of beer-drinking peoples, people in the Greek and Roman empires still prefer wine, seeing beer as the inferior drink of the 'barbarians'.

600 AD – During an outbreak of plague, St Arnold of Metz persuades people to drink beer in place of water (which was impure). The plague disappears.

793 – The foundations are laid for Ye Olde Fighting Cocks in St Albans, which claims to be the oldest pub in Britain.

822 – First documented mention of hops being used for brewing – Abbot Adalard of Corbie writes instructions that a tenth of wild hops gathered should be given to the porter of the monastery to make beer.

1040 – Brewing begins at Weihenstephan monastery in Germany. Today, Weihenstephan claims to be the oldest brewery in the world still in operation.

1400s – Monks in Bavaria develop the method of storing their beer in cold caves. Over time, this cold storage method inadvertently develops bottom-fermenting lager yeast.

1500s – As the Protestant Reformation spreads through Europe, so does the use of hops in beer (since the Catholic church taxed the botanicals used in herbal beer known as 'gruit').

1516 – William IV, Duke of Bavaria, decrees that across Bavaria 'the only ingredients used for the brewing of beer must be barley, hops and water' (yeast was not yet understood as a separate ingredient). In 1906, an updated version of this 'purity order' is applied across all of Germany, where it is still in place today.

1575 – In Germany, Heinrich Knaust publishes the first book on brewing, which includes descriptions of around 150 beers.

1620 – The pilgrims on the Mayflower land in Massachusetts instead of continuing south to a warmer location; one of the reasons for this is that they're running out of beer on the boat.

1632 – The Dutch West India Company opens the first commercial brewery in America. They did it so the settlers on the island of Manhattan would spend their time developing the land instead of brewing their own beer.

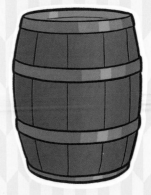

1703 – The term 'pale ale' first appears in England since the use of coke (a new smokeless fuel) in the malting process allows for lighter roasted malts.

1740s–1760s – Beer is seen as part of the solution to London's out-of-control gin problem. Tax laws begin to favour beer over gin, leading to a decrease in drunkenness and an increase in the standard of living in London.

1759 – Arthur Guinness signs a 9000-year lease for the St James's Gate Brewery, Dublin at a fixed rent of £45 per year. (Though the Guinness company will later buy out the property when the brewery outgrows its original four acres.)

1790 – James Squire, a convict sent on the First Fleet, becomes the first brewer in Australia, and in 1806 the first to successfully cultivate hops in Australia. At his death, the *Sydney Gazette* stated, 'As one of the primary inhabitants of the Colony ... none ever more exerted himself for the benefits of the inhabitants ...'

1814 – The collapse of a fermenting vat in Horse Shoe Brewery causes the London Beer Flood – a 300,000 gallon wave of porter breaks the back wall of the brewery and rushes into the immediate area, killing eight people.

1822 – The British East India Company asks Samuel Allsop, a brewer from Burton upon Trent, to brew pale ales for them to export to India. The bitter pale ales from Burton soon become known as 'India ales' or 'India pale ales'.

1842 – In the city of Pilsen, Josef Groll brews the first true pale lager (later known as a Czech pilsner). This clean-drinking style sparks an explosion of popularity for pale lagers across Europe and, later, the world.

1876 – Louis Pasteur publishes his book *Studies in Beer*. His scientific work in both the fields of fermentation and food hygiene are instrumental to beer becoming a viable commercial product.

1920 – Prohibition begins in the US, which sees many smaller beer producers go out of business. Even after Prohibition is lifted in 1933, there's a decades-long decline of beer diversity and local beer culture in America; by 1983, six mega-breweries control 92% of beer production in the US, and there are only 80 active breweries across the US.

1965 – In San Francisco, Fritz Maytag buys 51% of the failing Anchor Brewing because he enjoys its steam ale. Over the next decade, he improves the beer and the brewery; Anchor comes to thrive by brewing a diversity of styles in a market saturated with mass-produced lager, inspiring other brewers to do the same.

1971 – In the UK, four friends start the Campaign for the Revitalisation of Real Ale (later shortened to 'Campaign for Real Ale') with the aim of promoting and protecting cask ale and local pubs. In 2009, CAMRA reaches 100,000 members and almost doubles this number over the next decade.

1978 – Home brewing is federally legalised in the US for the first time since Prohibition. This leads to an explosion of people across America experimenting with beer styles other than pale lagers – a key part of the craft beer movement.

1981 – Sierra Nevada Brewing Company opens in California. Their pioneering pale ale – inspired by malty English pale ales but with boosted alcohol content, higher bitterness and loaded with American Cascade hops for flavour – is widely credited as beginning the American pale ale style.

1983 – Yakima Brewing and Malting Company releases the first beer labelled an 'India Pale Ale' in the American craft beer era.

1985 – The number of breweries in the US reaches 100. As microbreweries take off, this number will reach 1000 in 1996, and by 2022 there will be more than 9000 operating breweries in America.

1990 – Aroma hop HBC 394 is first bred. After almost two decades of trials, it's released to the brewing world in 2008 as Citra. With its intense aromas and citrussy flavour profile, Citra will go on to become the most popular aroma hop in the world.

1993 – The Ballarat University College and Royal Agricultural Society of Victoria join to run the first international beer and brewing competition in Australia. Today, the Australian International Beer Awards is the largest annual beer competition in the world with more than 2500 entries from 420 breweries in 21 countries.

1994 – The hop breeding program at Hop Products Australia crosses Australian variety Pride of Ringwood with German variety Perle. The resulting hop variety will be released as Galaxy in 2009, and have one of the highest concentrations of essential oils known in hops.

1995 – Goose Island's Bourbon County Stout is disqualified from the

Great American Beer Festival since it doesn't fit any of the style categories. Bourbon County went on to popularise bourbon barrel-aged stouts around the world.

2001 – After watching a TV chef add pepper to a soup in small increments while it simmers, brewer Sam Calagione pioneers the continuous hopping method. Dogfish Head's 90 Minute IPA is born.

2002 – As bitter IPAs grow in popularity, Stone Brewing releases Ruination, the first year-round packaged west coast double IPA. The race for breweries to out-bitter each other is far from over; in 2010, Danish brewer Mikkeller will release an IPA theoretically containing 1000 IBUs (International Bitterness Units), compared with Ruination's 100+.

2004 – A Vermont brewpub called The Alchemist releases its first batch of a double IPA called Heady Topper. It's unlike anything else on the market: explosively fruity yet extremely dank, boozy and bitter yet smooth, and hazy rather than clear. Heady Topper attracts a cult following with its own black market – brewpub customers sneak glasses of the stuff into the bathrooms and pour it into bottles they can smuggle out. This is the beer credited with sparking the haze craze.

2006 – Mikkeller is founded as a nomad brewing company in Denmark. Though they have no brewery of their own, they win an international competition with Beer Geek Breakfast and receive an international distribution deal the same year.

2007 – Ray Daniels founds the Cicerone Certification Program, a series of training courses and exams to improve knowledge and service in the beer industry. Cicerones are the sommeliers of the beer world – certified beer experts who have learned and tasted their way through many aspects of beer and use their knowledge and skills to lead others through the world of beer.

2008 – The first in-person meeting of the Pink Boots Society takes place at the Craft Brewers Conference in San Diego. The Pink Boots Society encourages and supports women in the beer industry. Today, they have chapters in USA, Canada, South America, Australia, NZ and Europe.

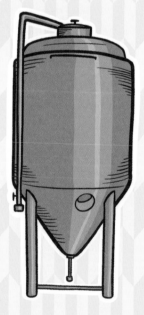

2009 – Scottish brewery Brewdog releases a 32% ABV beer to take the title of 'world's strongest beer' from German brewery Schorschbräu. This fuels a back-and-forth struggle between the two breweries for the title, culminating in a collaboration beer in 2020 – a 57.8% ABV beer called Strength in Numbers.

2011 – AB InBev, a multinational drinks company, purchases Goose Island Beer Co. In the following years, with big brewers getting into the craft beer market around the world with their own 'crafty' beers and by buying craft breweries, the language of 'independent breweries' becomes more prominent.

2014 – Beer writer Lars Marius Garshol visits traditional brewers in western Norway and is blown away by kveik, unique yeast strains with incredible properties that have been cultured for thousands of years in regional Norway. Over the next several years, Garshol works to introduce the rest of the world to kveik.

2015 – Sabro hops are commercially released and quickly become known for their distinct coconut flavour. Sabro is one of the hop varieties to popularise *neomexicanus* hops, a subspecies of hops that had been discovered growing wild in the mountains of New Mexico.

2016 – A London brewery makes a beer with a yeast culture swabbed from the wood of Roald Dahl's writing chair. (This is basically Jurassic Park but with beer instead of dinosaurs.)

2022 – Beer writer Mick Wüst coins the phrase, 'Jurassic Park but with beer instead of dinosaurs.'

Beer today

It's time for us to get a glimpse of where beer and the beer industry are at today. And the first thing to notice is that not all breweries are the same, and not all beer is the same.

Macro beer

Also known as 'commercial beer', 'mass-produced', 'the multi-nationals' or 'the Big Boys'.

Walk into a supermarket-owned retailer and these are the beers that take up 75% to 95% of the beer section. They're almost all pale lagers. They're the beer ads you saw on TV when you were a kid. They're the beers you saw people drinking when you were growing up. (Hopefully it was adults you saw drinking them, not other kids.) I'd bet good money that your first beer was one of these. And I'd double down and say you've had countless of them since.

Through the 20th century, beer became a mass-produced product in a way it had never been before. Plenty of factors led us to this point – pasteurisation, the Industrial Revolution, Prohibition, the rise of marketing, globalisation, the growth of capitalism – and the result is a beer market dominated by huge breweries owned by huge corporations, making huge volumes of lager and distributing it as widely as possible.

Since they pump out hundreds of millions of litres per year, everything they do happens on an enormous scale. Tweaking a recipe to save 1c per can or bottle can make them millions in profits – but it could also seriously annoy millions of loyal drinkers if they don't like the change. They can't risk having any inconsistency between batches, so they automate their processes as much as possible to minimise human error. They have long-term strategies for the way they source ingredients. They prioritise shelf life and stability because their product needs to travel across the country, sit in warehouses and still taste the way their dedicated drinkers have come to expect.

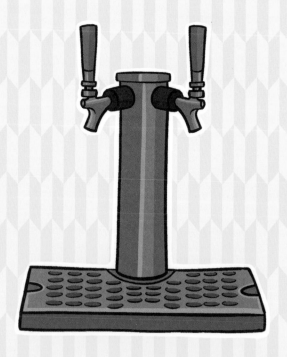

This is a world of market share and sales figures and tap contracts and marketing campaigns.

Unfortunately, by treating beer in this way for decades, the big boys have thrown up a bunch of negative side effects for beer along the way. By making beer as cheap as possible rather than focusing on flavour, macrobreweries have given beer (and lager in particular) the reputation of being an inferior drink associated with drunken louts and street brawls. And by focusing in on one very narrow portion of the spectrum of beer styles, they've convinced the world that beer is one-dimensional – 'beer flavoured'. Blasphemy!

But don't go getting the impression that these big companies don't know their beer. They have incredible technology and brilliant experts who have forgotten more about making beer than many others know. Their beers taste exactly the same whether you're drinking a pint in a small-town pub or buying a 6-pack that's been sitting on the shelf of a huge chain store for a year – and that's impressive. They may not be pushing boundaries or experimenting with new styles every week, but these breweries are excellent at pumping out easy-drinking, consistent and faultless lager.

Craft beer

What is craft beer? Depends who you ask! Everyone seems to have a slightly different idea.

If I had to sum it up, I'd say craft beer is for people who want more flavour and variety from their beer.

The craft beer movement started in the USA in the 1980s in direct opposition to mass-produced lagers, which had saturated the American market. Beer had become monochromatic.

As more and more Americans visited Europe, beer lovers and brewers discovered a diversity of styles, colours and flavours that blew their minds. In Germany, their eyes were opened to what lager could be, and they found a wealth of flavoursome ales in places like Belgium and the UK.

When these beer lovers headed back to the States, they couldn't contain their excitement. So they got brewing. Some brewed as a hobby, while others brewed professionally. Some made the traditional styles they'd fallen in love with, while others put their own twist on the beers. But they all found themselves sharing with others, wanting to introduce more people to the wide world of beer.

Thus began the craft beer movement. It started in the US, but it didn't stay there; the following decades saw it spread across continents. Breweries popped up at an unprecedented rate around the world – from Canada to Australia, from Denmark to South Africa, from Japan to New Zealand, from Ireland to Brazil. Across the globe, beer was beginning to take its rightful place in the eyes of millions, shining as a versatile and high-quality product made by skilled artisans.

The campaign for real ale

Across the pond, another movement sprung up in opposition to macrobreweries.

In 1971, four friends were worried about the state of beer in the UK. The rise of mass-produced keg beer had led to the decline of the flavoursome cask-conditioned ale they'd grown up with and was threatening the local pubs that served as community hubs.

To promote and protect cask ale – 'real ale' they called it – and UK pub culture, they started the Campaign for Real Ale (CAMRA). They printed their own newspaper, started a beer festival and campaigned to government, all with the aim of ensuring they didn't lose what they loved. It was partly about cultural heritage, and partly about making sure they could walk into a thriving pub and drink a tasty beer on a Friday night!

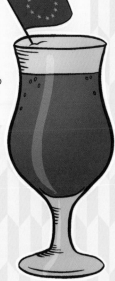

CAMRA started with four people in 1971, but 50 years on it's the largest consumer group in Europe, boasting almost 200,000 members.

Craft beer isn't easy to define. But it's generally agreed to be some combination of the following ...

Craft beer is made by people who see brewing as a craft, rather than just a means to make money. For these brewers, brewing is more than just a job – it's an art form. They'll put the craftsmanship of their beer first even when it's less cost effective. They like to educate their customers, and help them connect with the beer they're drinking. Talk to the owner of a craft brewery and it's easy to see that passion drives what they do.

Craft beer is focused on flavour. Brewers explore and showcase how different ingredients taste. They play with the range of styles available and what makes each one unique.

When multinational brewing companies advertise their lagers, they often describe them as 'cold', 'refreshing', 'crisp' and 'thirst-quenching'. Do you see a pattern? They don't talk about flavour! Many of these breweries only make low-flavour commercial lagers because it's easy to drink more of them – and sell more of them. But for craft breweries, selling as many litres of beer as possible isn't their only goal. They want to make brash IPAs, bold stouts and lagers with distinct character.

Compare rustic sourdough to white supermarket bread, or wood-fired pizza to the pizzas from the big chain restaurants. Just like these artisan products, craft beer takes longer to make and costs more, but it's full of flavour and it's worth it.

Craft beer is innovative, experimental and constantly evolving. While craft brewers love to rediscover traditional styles and brewing methods, they're not bound by any of them. They're mavericks. They seek out new ingredients and develop new styles. They try out new processes ('What if we used yoghurt to sour this beer?'; 'What if we aged an IPA in a bourbon barrel?'). They'll even mess around with weird and wonderful ingredients to make a salted caramel stout, a lavender saison or a bubblegum sour. They push boundaries and take risks that allow them to discover things they never would have discovered by playing it safe.

Craft beer is built on a sense of community. It creates a kind of fandom, where complete strangers can become friends based on a common interest: 'You like beer? I like beer!' Drinkers form groups on social media, bump into the same people at beer events, and get to know their local brewers and bar staff.

And it's not just the customers. Craft brewers often see each other as peers and allies rather than rivals or competitors – after all, they have the same goal of making excellent beer and sharing it with the world. They help each other out, share ingredients and equipment with each other, and collaborate on beers.

Craft beer celebrates 'local'. This isn't a product that comes out of some hidden factory. Craft breweries have a connection to a place and invite others to join them. They have taprooms you can come drink at – and bring your family to – so you get to know the people who make your beer. They celebrate drinking beer fresh from the source. They look after their regulars and welcome their feedback. They support charities and sponsor sports teams in their area. They host community events. They support and work with other local businesses and use local produce and ingredients where possible.

Craft beer is made in small(er) breweries. Many craft breweries start with one or two people. They may be working on the brewery part-time while they do their other job, or they may be the sole employees working around the clock. They may be using their own small tanks, or they may be using other breweries' equipment until they can afford some of their own.

'Small' is a relative term – some craft breweries only make 600 litres at a time, but there are also craft breweries that brew millions of litres a year. This might sound different to your idea of a microbrewery, but even a craft brewery that's grown to such a size is a big fish in a small pond; compare it to the macrobrewery whales and you'll see why it still fits in the craft category.

Craft beer is made by independent companies. For a lot of drinkers, the question of who owns a brewery matters. Many craft breweries are owned by a family or a few friends who started the business as a passion project, while others have investors who help the brewery grow. This is a world apart from a brewery owned by a giant corporation for which beer is just one of their interests.

Some people avoid the term 'craft beer' and instead talk about beer made by small breweries (implying careful attention to detail), local breweries (implying they're part of the community) or independent breweries (implying a passionate and personal approach to brewing). They're mostly talking about the same part of the beer industry, even if they're emphasising different aspects.

Like I said, craft beer isn't easy to define. But we don't always have to define it. Sometimes it's okay to just drink the beer you want to drink.

Home brewing

Most of us have tasted beer brewed at home – either you've made it yourself or you've tasted someone else's home brewed beer.

How was it? Was it bad? A lot of home brewing is. Making good beer is hard work, and there's plenty that can go wrong – among other things, beer can get infected with unwanted bacteria and get a sour taste, and poor temperature control can cause the yeast to make undesirable flavours. I've tasted more bad home brew than good home brew.

But there's no real reason home brewing can't be great. Many of the best brewers in the world started by making beer in their kitchen at home.

There's a difference in scale and level of technology between home brewing and professional brewing, but most of the elements are the same. You need to be able to clean your equipment. You need a way to heat water for an extended period of time. You need a vessel for heating and another vessel for fermenting. And you need a way to store your beer when it's ready.

There are almost limitless options to what a home brew set-up could look like, depending on how much money you want to spend and how much you want to streamline your process. A good strategy is to start cheap to see if you like it.

A low-tech version could be a 10 L pot on the stove, a plastic fermenting vessel from a home brew shop, and a bunch of empty soft drink bottles. Cheap as chips, but your brew day is going to involve a lot of hard work and mess.

If you're keen to pimp your set-up, you could spend a few hundred dollars for a mid-tech version: a big boil kettle to sit on your gas burner, a grain bag, a decent fermenter, a bunch of bottles, a cheap secondhand fridge for temperature control during fermentation … basically, you can upgrade any areas of the set-up to help things run smoothly and give you more control over the process.

If you like your gadgets and are happy to shell out for the best toys, there are high-tech home brew kits that remove much of the friction. You can easily spend upwards of a thousand dollars on an all-in-one brewing system. You can buy a grain mill to crush your own malt. You can invest in a fermenting fridge and a beer fridge, and get a couple of kegs to keep your beer in.

Then there are people who'll bring in an angle grinder and welding iron and custom build their own mini-brewery out of kegs. It ends up looking like a car from Mad Max. These home brewers usually have a home bar with a few beer taps too. You want to be friends with these people.

When it comes to ingredients, again there's a range of ways you can go. You can grab easy options, or you can do hours of research and become friends with the person at the local home brew store. It all depends on how much attention you want to devote to the hobby, and why you're brewing in the first place: do you want cheap booze, or are you on a lifelong pursuit to brew the perfect beer?

These are your three main options for home brewing:

- **Beer concentrate kit** – tins of hopped malt extract (a thick, concentrated liquid) that make up the basis of a brew.
The home brewer just mixes this with brewing sugar and water and pitches the yeast to make the beer. Easy as anything.

- **Fresh wort kit** – a volume of wort (say, 15 L) that's been professionally brewed from grain. It's already hopped, and it's ready to go. All the home brewer needs to do is ferment it.

- **All grain** – This is making beer completely from scratch, using the same kinds of ingredients a professional brewer uses. In a perfect world, all beer would be brewed this way. But not everyone has the time, the space, the skill or the equipment for all grain brewing.

Home brew kits come with instructions and recipes that, when followed exactly, will result in the intended beer style. But when home brewers gain enough confidence, they can level-up their brews by finding new recipes online or beginning to experiment on their own. Combining concentrate kits, dry-hopping for extra aroma, adding specialty malts for colour and flavour, using different yeast … there are plenty of ways to change the final product.

This is a hobby to take up at your own risk. It's easy to catch the bug.

If you start brewing beer at home, you'll fall into one of three camps: you'll brew once or twice, then let it slide as life gets busy; you'll become an avid home brewer that keeps going further down the rabbit hole; or you'll become a professional brewer.

Beer around the world

If you're anything like me, you're intimately familiar with your own part of the world, slightly familiar with the places you've travelled to, and woefully ignorant of just about everywhere else. Perhaps the most important thing we can do when thinking about beer culture is to look around and realise how little we know, so we don't fall into the trap of thinking everywhere is the same. Because there's rich variety in beer culture around the world.

In America, it can look like touring a region's brewpubs to find your favourite burger and IPA combo, or sinking suds in a cheap and cheerful dive bar. Bottoms up!

In Mexico, it can look like picking up a couple of *caguamas* (large beer bottles nicknamed 'sea turtles') on a hot day, or drinking your beer as a *michelada* (with added lime juice and assorted spicy sauces) in a salt-rimmed glass. Salud!

In Ireland, it can look like heading down to the local for a cold stout, warm stew, and lively tunes on the fiddle and flute. Sláinte!

In England, it can look like soaking in the ambience of a local pub, with the bartender pulling pints from a hand pump and the football playing in the background. Chin-chin!

In Belgium, it can look like settling in a corner of a dingy cafe with a huge selection of beer styles, or buying beer made by Trappist monks directly from the monastery. Schol!

In Germany, it can look like pushing through a crowded beer hall during Oktoberfest, relaxing with a stein in a sunny beer garden, or walking down the street with a *wegbier* ('journey beer'). Prost!

In South Africa, it can look like gathering around the fire with a *tjop* and *dop* (a wood-fired barbecue chop and a drink), having a traditional style of beer made with drought-resistant sorghum or cassava, or exploring the growing craft beer scene. Gesondheid!

In Australia, it can look like going to the nearest brewery or pub to knock back a few schooners (because the first one didn't touch the sides), get stuck into a parmi, and chat with strangers like they're your new best friends. Cheers!

In Japan, it can look like starting with a round of beers at a tiny *izakaya* (dine-in bar) before you eat, or grabbing a beer from a vending machine. Kanpai!

In Vietnam, it can look like sitting in the streets being served *bia hoi* ('fresh beer') straight from the keg – some of the cheapest beer you'll find anywhere in the world. Dzô!

I love gaining a little insight into different cultures. If nothing else, it can help me plan my next beer holiday.

Ingredients

You could walk up to anyone on the street and ask them what's in wine, and every single one will say 'grapes'. Ask them about cider, they'll tell you 'apples'. But ask them what's in beer and half of them will give you confused silences and random guesses. The ingredients of beer are a mystery to most people.

So let me clear it up for you. What makes beer look and smell and taste like it does? Water, malt, hops, yeast. That refreshing pale gold lager that smells like lemon? Water, malt, hops, yeast. That cloudy German wheat beer that reminds you of banana bread? Water, malt, hops, yeast. That shining ruby IPA that's all sticky toffee and pine needles? Water, malt, hops, yeast. That black stout that drinks like a thick mocha? Water, malt, hops, yeast. That doesn't mean it's simple, though. There are four ingredients, but there are endless possibilities.

Of course, life would be no fun if everyone played by the rules. Some styles of beer include other ingredients, and brewers will sometimes play with interesting adjuncts. But water, malt, hops and yeast are the main things that determine what a beer will be like.

Reinheitsgebot

There's a 500-year-old law in Germany that says brewers can use only water, malt, hops and yeast in beer.

Reinheitsgebot – the 'purity order' – was passed in 1516 in Bavaria, and since 1906 it's been in place across Germany.

Reinheitsgebot has evolved slightly over the years, but the modern law still carries the spirit of the purity order. It's as if Germany is saying, 'We make great beer. Don't mess with it.'

Water

It's hard to get excited about water. It's one of those basic essentials that most of us in the western world take for granted. But water is the stuff of life. And it's also the stuff of beer. (Does this prove 'beer = life'? More research needed.)

Most of our planet is covered with water, and the human body is made up of around 60% water – or 75% if you're a baby.

(You're probably not, though.) But most beers are made up of over 90% water. That makes it a very important ingredient to brewers.

We often think of water as pure H_2O, but in reality, it always contains traces of other things. Pond water, for example, is high in organic matter ranging from algae to dead fish to women falsely accused of being witches. Water from underground springs is largely witch-free but may be full of minerals that have dissolved in it as it flowed over and filtered through different kinds of rock. Water high in minerals is considered 'hard' and low in minerals is called 'soft'. These different amounts and kinds of minerals can shape how beer tastes and feels in the mouth, making different water profiles more or less suited to various styles of beer.

Have a look at some of the famous beer locations of the world ...

London is a city with a hard water supply because of all the limestone and chalky rock. This could be a disaster for brewers ... unless you counter the harshness of the water with the robustness of dark malts. Say hello to London's reputation for porters! (A similar quirk of geography helped Dubliners develop their stouts.)

To the uninitiated, **Burton upon Trent** may sound like one guy sitting on another guy's shoulders, but it's actually a town in England that became famous for its bitter pale ales. Thanks to gypsum in local aquifers, the town's mineral-rich water gives a dry finish to beers and amps up the hop bitterness. (San Diego also has hard water, which plays into the city's penchant for dry, bitter IPAs.)

In the 1840s, the city of **Pilsen** hired Josef Groll to brew a lager to challenge the lagers of Munich. He did an excellent job of snagging some Munich yeast, using impressive new pale malt and choosing local hops ... but he can't take credit for Pilsen having some of the softest water in the world. He made the first pilsner, a clean and subtle beer that became the grandparent of pale lagers all around the globe.

Nowadays, brewers aren't entirely bound by their location and local water supply, nor do they need to airlift giant buckets of soft water from Pilsen every time they want to make a pilsner.

They can strip unwanted matter out of water, change the acidity, and add desirable minerals to exactly the levels they're after. Brewers can design their own water profile – and even copy the profile of Munich's or Pilsen's water if they want to replicate a city's signature style.

Remember, beer is over 90% water. If the water's not right, the beer won't be right.

Malt

Malt is an impressive ingredient. It's responsible for the colour of beer, giving a pilsner its shining straw colour and an imperial stout its blacker-than-night darkness. It's responsible for the body of a beer – whether it feels light in the mouth, or thick and heavy. It can add weight to a session ale, lighten a lager or help foam stick around for longer. It's the difference between the dry finish of a west coast IPA and the chewy caramel sweetness of a red IPA.

The amount and kind of malt affects how much alcohol is in a beer.

Then there's the flavour – bread, or biscuits, or toffee, or chocolate, or smoke …

There's a lot to thank malt for.

What is malt?

There's an old military quote by Napoleon that says, 'An army marches on its stomach'. He knew even the best general can't win a war without the right food to feed his soldiers. Well, if the brewer is a general and the yeast are soldiers, then the food they need is malt.

Malted grains are to beer what grapes are to wine and what apples are to cider; they provide the sugars that yeast eat to make fermentation happen. But while the sugars in grapes and apples are ready to feed the yeast from the moment the fruit is harvested, malt is the result of a magical process that turns unfermentable grain into prime yeast food. And the magicians who turn that grain into malt are called maltsters.

To make malt, maltsters start with raw grain – usually barley, but wheat, oats and rye can also play the part. Grains are amazing things. Each kernel is a little plant-growing engine, containing everything it needs to grow from a tiny seed to a blossoming plant.

But maltsters are tricksters. They soak the grains in water to convince them it's time to start growing, so the grains begin to break down their starches into simple sugars. Then BAM – the maltster dries the grains in a kiln to stop the sugars from being used up. These grains will never get to grow into a plant. But don't feel too sorry for the little fellas – they're now malt and will get to give their sugar to make beer instead.

Different kinds of malt

Skilled maltsters also use the kiln to do what ovens do best – cook food to perfection. They can toast or roast the malt until it's exactly as they want it, producing all kinds of different malts – even from the same grain. A brewer might then use one kind of malt or several kinds in a single beer, depending on what they're going for.

Pale malts are like bread toasted at the lowest setting on a toaster. They're the light-coloured malts that make a straw-coloured lager or a yellow pale ale, and can help a beer remain light-bodied and easy to drink. Pale malts bring flavours of baked goods like bread or biscuits. But with light colour comes light taste, and a brewer can hide the character of pale malts easily enough if they want.

Toasted and roasted malts are like darker toast, cooked until it's brown or even black. Brewers can use a tiny amount to add a touch of gold and introduce some toasty or nutty notes to a beer, or they can use more to make dark beers and hit you with flavours of chocolate or coffee or raisins.

Maltsters caramelise some of the sugars in the grain to make decadent **caramel and crystal malts**. In small amounts, they add a glint of gold or red to a beer; in larger amounts, they bring deep gold or ruby hues, sweet flavours of toffee or caramel or dried fruits, and a sticky or syrupy body.

In the old days, all malt was smoky since the kilning process used open fires. Nowadays, **smoked malt** isn't used in many beers, but a brewer can choose to use some to add a touch of wood smoke or make a full-on bacon bomb.

Malted barley isn't the only grain that can be used in beer – **other malts and grains** come in handy too. Wheat can add body and increase head retention. Oats can make a beer smooth or even creamy, which is great in a stout or hazy IPA. Rye has a spicy character that works well in some styles. Rice and corn can give a drier, crisper feel in the mouth. Sometimes grains are even left unmalted to bring different characteristics to a brew – most commonly wheat, oats, and roasted barley.

Hops

Hops are the sexiest ingredient in beer today. They're the celebrities, the rockstars, the cool kids of the beer world. They're mentioned in beer names, pictured on label art, and gushed over in tasting notes.

What are hops?

Imagine a vineyard, with its rows of vines growing along parallel wires. Now imagine these rows of plants don't grow horizontally, but grow upwards on trellises, creating six-metre-tall bushy columns of plant. Now imagine that instead of bunches of grapes, you find small cones growing all over the plant, like tiny pinecones made of green leafy petals.

These cones are hops, the flowering fruit of the *Humulus lupulus* plant from the Cannabaceae family. (Yes, hops are related to cannabis. No, you shouldn't try to smoke them.) They're full of precious acids and oils that give beer so much of its distinctive and delicious flavour.

Hops are only harvested once a year, but because those good bits start breaking down within hours of the hops being picked, the majority of hops are immediately dried or otherwise processed so they last year round.

Hops do three main things in beer ...

- **They're a natural preservative.** Along with alcohol, the acids in hops help to keep nasties out of your beer so it doesn't spoil.

- **They add bitterness.** This makes beer an acquired taste, but it's also to thank for the complexity and more-ish-ness of beer. Hop bitterness acts as a counterbalance to malt sweetness (and vice versa).

- **They add aroma and flavour.** The aromatic oils in hops can bring a huge spectrum of fun smells and tastes to beer. Is your beer fruity? Floral? Piney? Grassy? That's the hops. (Sometimes craft brewers add fruit to beer, but usually it's the hops. No one's adding grass to beer.) Brewers can use a single hop variety in a beer to get a distinct flavour or several for more complex hop character.

Different varieties, different flavours

While people have been using hops to preserve beer for over a thousand years, the focus on distinct aromas and flavours is a more modern approach, both for hop breeders and for brewers.

The so-called Old World varieties tend to be more subtle and show earthy, spicy, herbal and floral characters. Meanwhile, New World varieties aren't interested in subtlety; they're prized for their bold fruity and piney aromatics that get all up in your face.

There are over 300 varieties of hops grown and used in beer around the world, with more popping up all the time. Just like with grapes, hops taste different based on the soil and climate, meaning hop growing regions around the globe have reputations for growing different kinds of hops.

North America

Known for: punchy fruit and resinous flavours
Examples: Cascade helped bring in the modern hop era in the 1970s and 1980s; Citra, with its massive citrussy personality, is the most popular hop variety in the world; Mosaic can bring mango, pine, berries or candied fruit depending on how it's used; Sabro is one of a new family of hops called *neomexicanus* and can bring coconut and mint flavours and even a creamy mouthfeel to a beer.

Germany & Czech Republic

Known for: delicate spicy, earthy and floral flavours
Examples: Hallertau Mittelfrüh, Spalt, Tettnang and Saaz are known as the four noble hops, and their subtle characteristics make excellent traditional lagers; Mandarina Bavaria and Huell Melon are part of Germany's foray into fruity New World hops.

England

Known for: delicate spicy, earthy and woody notes
Examples: Fuggle and East Kent Golding are both great in a bitter or English pale ale, but Fuggle is known for its earthy notes and soft spice, while EKG can bring lavender, honey and thyme.

Australia & New Zealand

Known for: bright bursts of tropical fruit

Examples: Galaxy won the hearts of many when Australian brewery Stone & Wood popularised its passionfruit tang; Riwaka and Motueka are both New Zealand hops that have Saaz as a parent but shun its subtlety, instead shining with tropical fruits and citrus.

All these varieties are the same species of hop, just as chihuahuas, pitbulls and St Bernards are all the same species of dog. But the spectrum of hop characters includes flavour descriptions of resin, spice, citrus blossoms, melon, lime, strawberry, coconut, bourbon barrel, passionfruit, cedar, ripe pawpaw, black pepper, white grapes …

… all from the humble hop.

Yeast

Get a brewer talking about yeast and you'll be there for a while. At times, they'll talk about yeast in the scientific language of microbiology; at other times, they'll talk about it like it's a mystical, magical creature. While everything else in the brewing process is so precise and controllable, yeast manages to keep an air of mystery around it – and brewers respect that.

A brewer once said to me, 'I don't make beer. I make sweet, bitter water. It's the yeast that makes the beer.'

What is yeast, and what does it do?

Do you want the textbook answer or the fun answer?

Textbook answer: yeast are single-celled organisms in the fungus kingdom. The most common species used in brewing are *Saccharomyces cerevisiae* (ale yeast) and *Saccharomyces pastorianus* (lager yeast).

Fun answer: yeast are the tiny monsters that make the booze and bubbles in beer.

These tiny monsters are responsible for fermentation. They make bread rise, they turn grape juice into wine, and they turn malty, hoppy water into beer. They do this by chewing on sugar, burping up carbon dioxide and spitting out alcohol.

Because yeast *want* to eat sugar, people could make alcoholic drinks long before they knew yeast existed or understood how fermentation worked. But skilled brewers know how to keep these little beasties happy, which makes for better tasting beer. They do this by looking after the yeast like you'd look after babies – keep them clean, feed them and keep them the right temperature.

Keep them clean. There are all kinds of other microorganisms who'd love to get into beer to eat the sugar before the yeast, so a huge part of a brewer's job is to keep the brewing equipment clean, clean, clean to keep the nasties out and protect their precious yeast babies. (Some brewers call themselves 'janitors who farm yeast on the side'.)

Feed them. Yeast can be fussy, so brewers want to give them plenty of sugar they can eat. This includes choosing the malts, extracting the right amounts of sugars from the malt, and sometimes adding other kinds of sugars too.

Keep them the right temperature. If the yeast get too cool, they won't multiply, thrive and ferment properly. If they get too warm, they get stressed and start making by-products that change the flavour of the beer.

Different kinds of yeast

Ale vs lager. There are many strains of yeast used in brewing, but they almost all come under the same two species in the yeast family tree: ale yeast or lager yeast. (The small amount of beers that don't fit these two categories use wild yeast.)

Ale yeasts and lager yeasts ferment differently – ale yeast rises to the top of the tank and ferments at warmer temperatures, while lager yeast sinks to the bottom of the tank and ferments at cooler temperatures – but they can both be used to produce a range of beer styles and flavours.

Neutral vs distinctive. For many kinds of beer, brewers want the yeast to do its fermenting without adding its own flavour to the brew. In this case, they use yeast strains that keep a low profile so the other ingredients can stand centre stage.

But for some beers, brewers want yeast strains that bring distinctive aromas and flavours to the table: the complex fruity character of an English ale yeast, the playful tropical aromas some strains add to hazy IPAs, or the citrussy and peppery notes of a Belgian saison yeast. Sometimes yeast is the hero, not the sidekick.

Commercial yeast strains vs wild yeast. The above examples are all isolated yeast strains – think of a plantation forest with one single species of pine. But most of our world is full of wild yeast, and nature isn't quite so neat – think of a forest with a variety of species of trees, and mosses, and flowers, and bushes and shrubs.

Nowadays, most brewers use isolated commercial yeast strains because they're more predictable and controllable. But there are also brewers who walk on the wild side – mad scientists who collect yeast samples from nature so they can experiment. It can be a gamble at times since they never know what microorganisms are going to show up in their beer, but these eccentric geniuses end up making some amazing creations. They're generally sour (the beers, not the people), and their complex flavours can range from fruity and floral to descriptors like 'horse blanket'. I once heard someone praising a beer for its 'wet sock' flavours.

Believe it or not, many discerning drinkers chase after these kinds of beers and will pay top dollar for them.

Yeast are tiny, yet the world of yeast is vast and complex – and perhaps my inability to stick to one metaphor helps to get that across. Are these microorganisms like mystical creatures, like tiny monsters or like babies? Like a forest or like superheroes?

Or perhaps yeast is more like the Illuminati – even when you can't see it at work, you get the sneaking suspicion it's behind everything ...

Other ingredients

Adding **fruit** to beer is nothing new. Belgian brewers have been using sour cherries to make kriek lambics and raspberries to make framboise lambics for centuries. Nowadays you see all kinds of fruited beers, from blueberry stouts to strawberry blonde ales to mango sours to grapefruit IPAs.

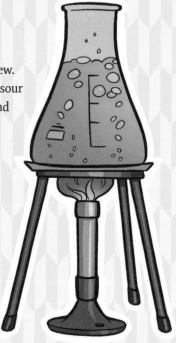

Coffee, chocolate and vanilla are all at home in the dark malty flavours of a porter or stout, and occasionally you'll see a vanilla pale ale or a coffee kölsch.

Different kinds of fermentable sugars can be used to boost the alcohol content of a beer. Some affect the flavour and colour; others are chosen because they don't.

Lactose is an unfermentable sugar derived from milk and can be used to add sweetness and body to beer. Once upon a time, you'd only see lactose in milk stouts, and only in small amounts. But its thick sweetness is now used to make vanilla milkshake IPAs, chocolatey pastry stouts and fruit smoothie sours. With novelty beers like

Double Vanilla Custard Pancake Imperial Nitro Thickshake IPA from Sydney's One Drop Brewing, we see that brewers like to have fun too.

Coriander seed and orange peel add a zesty freshness to Belgian witbier, while coriander seed and salt work together to give a crisp and more-ish character to gose.

All kinds of herbs, roots and spices are used to make gruit, an old style of beer from before hops were in common usage. Juniper? Liquorice? Chamomile? It's all fair game.

Oyster stouts are self-explanatory (though some of us would question why they exist in the first place).

I've seen beers that contain earl grey tea, hamburgers, seawater, croissants, cash, volcanic rocks, chicken carcasses and squid ink, and beers that have been fermented with the naturally occurring yeast from beards, Roald Dahl's armchair, belly buttons, and other sources that would make your granny blush.

The reality is that just about anything that *could* be put into a beer *has* been put into a beer. Of course, whether any particular ingredient *should* be put into a beer is another question entirely …

Brewers and the brewing process

Making beer is easy. Making good beer ... now that's another story.

Brewers are like chefs – they work with a recipe, put in the ingredients, stir and boil and taste to see if it's coming out the way they wanted it to.

But they're also part chemist. Brewers fiddle with the minerals in the water, monitor the amount of sugar that comes from the malt, adjust the acidity of the beer, watch the temperature of the beer during fermentation, measure the compounds that give bitterness, and track the chemical reactions happening throughout the brewing process.

They're also part microbiologist. Brewers need to know exactly what the yeast needs in order to ferment properly, and what to tweak or change when the yeast does something unexpected.

There's also a sliver of engineer in there. With all the equipment heating up, cooling down, pumping liquid through pipes and hoses and tanks, there are plenty of ways for things to go wrong.

And brewers are part janitor. They seem to spend most of their time cleaning – partly to keep any unwanted microorganisms out of the beer, and partly because slushy wet grain and splashed beer have a habit of getting everywhere and making things smell.

Sourcing ingredients, controlling temperatures, measuring oxygen levels, balancing flavours … getting the science right while also unleashing your inner artist and doing all the sweaty grunt work … okay, so making beer isn't easy. But brewers do it anyway, and I'm glad they do.

A non-brewer's guide to brewing

The brewing process is extremely technical. Over the years, I've had many brewers explain the details and the science to me, and for a long time it went in one ear and out the other. So many steps! So many weird words!

Brewers, like any experts, sometimes struggle to explain the process in ways that us non-experts can understand. They seem to speak a different language and can sometimes forget that normal people don't know what 'grist' and 'wort' and 'lautering' mean.

Eventually I went on enough brewery tours and asked enough stupid questions that I got my head around it and learned the language. Now I can talk about the process in a way my non-brewer brain understands.

So here's the brewing process in a nutshell. Not every brewery has the same equipment, not every brewer does things the same way, and not every kind of beer is made the same way. But it goes a little like this …

The brewing process

1
MILLING

Crack open the grains to get at the good stuff inside.

4
BOILING

Boil the wort to sterilise it (kill off unwanted bacteria and wild yeast), and add hops to give bitterness, flavour and aroma.

2
MASHING

Mix the malt with hot water to extract the sugars from the grains. This makes a thin, sweet porridge.

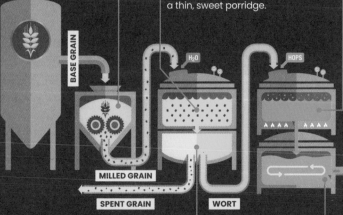

BASE GRAIN

H₂O

HOPS

MILLED GRAIN

SPENT GRAIN

WORT

HOT WORT

3
LAUTERING

Separate the liquid from the grain, rinse any remaining sugars off the grain, and get rid of the grain so you're left with wort (sweet malt water).

5
WHIRLPOOLING

Spin the liquid to get rid of all the little hop chunks. (Option of adding more hops here.)

7
FERMENTING

Add the yeast, which will munch the sugars, multiply, and make booze and bubbles (alcohol and carbon dioxide). This is where the magic happens – the wort turns into beer. (Option of adding even more hops here.)

PASTEURISING

Some breweries heat the beer for a short time to kill off remaining yeast and bacteria and improve shelf life. Some choose not to for maximum flavour.

8
FILTERING

Some breweries filter out small particles to make the beer super clear and improve shelf life. Some choose not to for maximum flavour.

9
COLD CONDITIONING/LAGERING

Chill the beer to near freezing and leave it there to smooth out the flavour and clarify the beer.

10
CARBONATING

Put bubbles (more CO_2) into the beer.

YEAST

DRY HOPS / SPICES

COOL WORT

CO_2

BRITE TANK

BEER BEER BEER BEER

BEER

BARREL AGEING

6
COOLING

Cool the bitter wort down to a temperature that's safe for yeast. But do it quickly, before other tiny beasties get in!

11
PACKAGING

Get the beer dressed up in its finest clothes, ready to meet the drinker – keg, bottle or can.

Packaging solutions

Kegs

Pros: cost effective, good for distribution, excellent at protecting beer from light and oxygen.

Cons: hard to fit in the door of your fridge at home or sneak to a picnic.

Bottles

Pros: portable, make a satisfying 'clink' sound when you cheers.

Cons: allow light and small amounts of oxygen into beer; require a bottle opener.

Cans

Pros: portable, easy to transport, excellent at protecting beer from light and oxygen.

Cons: don't 'clink' when you cheers them.

section two

I can't help but shudder when someone says all beers taste the same. It's like saying all fruit tastes the same. But lemons are totally different to bananas, raspberries taste nothing like watermelons and no one's slicing up tomato on their breakfast cereal. There's incredible variety in the world of beer – maybe more than with any other kind of drink. And it's just begging you to discover it.

Beer styles

There are well over a hundred different styles of beer, with a huge diversity of colour, flavour and alcohol strength. Knowing the style of a beer can give you an idea of what to expect from it before you drink it.

Judges of beer competitions have specific criteria they're looking for in each style (the BJCP Style Guidelines are available for free online). But for the rest of us, beer styles aren't hard and fast rules. In the same way you could argue with someone about the difference between a soup and a stew ('Stews have chunks!' 'But minestrone has chunks, and that's a soup!'), there's plenty of scope for discussion and debate about beer styles.

What's ABV?

ABV refers to 'alcohol by volume'. It measures the alcohol content of a drink as a percentage.

Three pints of a 4% ABV beer will contain exactly the same amount of alcohol as one pint of a 12% ABV beer. Beer maths is fun!

So what's light and what's heavy?

Here's my own unofficial key:

Beers **under 4% ABV** are light. You can have one or two and still drive or have a longer session on them while keeping your wits about you.

Beers around the **4% or 5% ABV** mark are steady drinkers. Have a few and you'll feel tipsy but should be fine.

Once you get up to **6% and 7% ABV**, you'll need to be careful. If you knock them down one after the other, they'll knock you right back.

Above 8% ABV, we're looking at thumpers. 10%? 12%? 14%? This is how strong wines are, and they serve those in 100ml glasses, not in cans four times that size. These beers are super flavoursome, but drinker beware.

Outside of competitions, there's no reason brewers have to follow styles or brew to specific rules. Sometimes they will brew according to style – for example, make a classic pilsner – but they also might play around and experiment with different ingredients and techniques to make a beer that doesn't fit neatly into a style.

It's impossible to describe every kind of beer that exists, but this section gives a rough roadmap you can use to start navigating the beer world. After that, it's up to you to explore.

Why is there no section for wheat beers?

Because I think that's a dumb category.

All kinds of beers include wheat as an ingredient, but they're worlds apart. Berliner weisses are sour, hefeweizens tastes like banana, American wheat ales are hoppy, and lambics are musty. Why on earth would we group these beers together? Just doesn't make sense to me. So I divided them up as I see fit. Enjoy finding them on your travels through this section!

Ales vs lagers

Just about every beer in the world today is a lager or an ale, depending on what kind of yeast was used to ferment it. (There is a third category – wild ales, which allow wild yeasts to ferment the beer – but it's much more niche.)

Ale has been around in one form or another for ages since ale yeasts are easily found in nature. They're survivors – tough little beasties that are happy to ferment at warmer and variable temperatures.

Lager is more of a newcomer, only around 600 years old; practically still a child. Lager yeasts are more delicate, wanting cooler temperatures in order to do their thing. In the wild, this kind of sensitivity doesn't get you very far. But thanks to a decree in 16th century Bavaria that only allowed brewing in winter, lagers got the chance to make their way onto the main stage.

Lager's time to shine

In Bavaria in the 1500s, they had a problem.

Beers brewed in winter tasted great, but beers brewed in summer often tasted terrible. Duke Albrecht V got fed up with this beer spoilage and decided to put an end to it: he decreed that beer could only be brewed in the cooler months. This improved beer quality across the board, and also inadvertently gave lager yeasts a leg up, since these strains fared better in the cooler temperature than ale yeasts.

Thanks to this unnatural selection, lager yeasts thrived and lager beers took off.

What's the difference?

The clearest delineation is whether a beer uses ale yeast or lager yeast. After that, it gets a little murkier.

Usually, there's a difference in the production. Ales are fermented warmer than lagers, and when they're ready, they're ready. Lagers are fermented at cooler temperatures, then are held for weeks at close to freezing temperature in a process called 'lagering' (the word 'lager' is German for 'storage', since lagerbier was stored cold in caves or cellars). During this time, sediment in the beer drops out of suspension to leave a clear brew and unwanted flavours fade away.

It's tempting to say there's a difference in taste. That lagers have a characteristic cleanness, while warmer-fermented ales are more likely to hold onto the by-product flavours of fermentation.

But this isn't always the case. Ales and lagers can both be clean tasting. They can both be high or lower alcohol and light or dark in colour depending on the malts. Ales aren't restricted to English real ales or hearty stouts or bitter IPAs or whatever you think of when you hear the word 'ale.' And lagers aren't restricted to the monochromatic low-flavour beers from the giant corporate breweries.

Pale lagers

Through the 20th century, pale lagers came to achieve what supervillains only dream of: world domination.

Breweries all over the globe pump out millions upon millions of litres of pale lager. Look at Budweiser and Coors, XXXX and VB, Heineken, Stella Artois, Carlsberg, Peroni, Corona, Beck's, Estrella Damm, Efes, Asahi, Tsingtao, Tiger, Singha, Kingfisher ... they're not exactly the same, but all these beers sit in the same narrow sliver of the beer spectrum.

This is why people sometimes ask for 'normal beer' or 'beer that tastes like beer'. It's because they grew up thinking that all beer was pale lager.

There are those who drink lagers exclusively (while knowing nothing about them), and others who refer to lager as 'fizzy yellow water'. But people in both of these camps are oversimplifying pale lagers. There's more to them than meets the eye.

Beers in the pale lager family all share a certain vibe, even when they're different styles. Their appearance obviously comes into it – they're all pale straw or gold in colour, and they're brilliantly clear and sparkle like a gemstone. But what really holds pale lagers together is their supreme drinkability. For the most part they're clean beers with a dry, crisp finish. Most are light in flavour, mild in bitterness and made with refreshment in mind. They're easy to drink and difficult to put down, and since the majority sit under 5%

ABV, they're light enough to be knocked back one after the other. This makes them perfect as a social drink – there's little more satisfying than sinking a few cold lagers on a hot day, laughing with your mates before pointing to an empty glass and asking, 'Another one?'

The first pale lager?

In the 1830s, the city of Pilsen in Bohemia (modern day Czech Republic) had a problem. The local ales were getting edged out by the imported lagers from neighbouring Bavaria.

Eventually, the leaders of Pilsen decided to fight lager with lager: they built a Bavarian-style brewery and brought in a Bavarian brewer named Josef Groll to brew lagers. But while Groll nabbed himself some Bavarian lager yeast, he didn't brew dark lagers made with wood-fired malt like they were doing in Munich. He took advantage of new malting technology to make paler malt than ever before. Combined with local Saaz hops and the extremely soft water of Pilsen, this made for a lager unlike the Bavarian lagers – blonde and bright, clean and crisp, with none of the smokiness of wood-fired malt.

In 1842, Josef Groll made what we would now call a Czech pilsner, and started a revolution of clean pale lagers that would span centuries and continents. And the world would never be the same.

Low flavour, easy to drink ... sounds like there's not much to these pale lagers. Does that mean they're easy to make?

Helles no.

Brewers see a well-made lager as the gold standard of brewing, and a way to show how skilled a brewer really is. They'll often say there's 'nowhere to hide' with a lager.

Have you ever splattered a bit of pasta sauce onto a colourful floral shirt? No one notices it. But that same tiny stain on a clean white shirt can be seen from a mile away. The same is true of a pale lager – since there's low malt and hop profile, the smallest fault stands out in a way that it might not in a hoppy ale or malty stout. So it's ab-so-lute-ly essential that the brewers treat the yeast with the greatest of care so they don't get any unwanted by-products during fermentation.

Large breweries employ microbiologists and lab technicians, spend millions on incredible equipment, and use high-tech filtration and pasteurisation to produce consistently flawless crystal clear lagers.

Small breweries don't have the same resources. When they put out a clean lager, it's due to painstaking effort by the brewer: pedantic cleaning, diligent temperature control and careful monitoring. Most small brewers won't filter their lagers, but will achieve clear lagers the old fashioned way – by lagering their beer in a tank for five to eight weeks (or longer). They'll also take pride in the fact that their lagers retain those delicate flavours that get killed off in the pasteurisation process.

Next time you taste a clean, crisp lager, think of the cost and effort that went into making it. A good lager is a testament to the skill of the brewer; even the most experimental or hop-crazy craft brewer will pay respect to a well-made lager.

Some kinds of pale lager

Pilsner

The O.G. of pale lagers. Pilsners made in the Czech style have a slightly sweet biscuity or bready taste, and the Saaz hops give a hop bitterness that's spicy without being aggressive. They're low in carbonation with a rounded mouthfeel.

A German-style pils will use hops like Tettnang or Hallertau, giving more of a lemony or honey taste. They'll generally have a drier, more bitter finish than Czech pilsners.

Helles

Helles means 'bright' or 'blonde' in German, as this style came about in Munich as a pale lager to rival pilsners. The hops in a helles give a bitterness to balance the malt, but it's the malt that brings the flavour – while it's still crisp, a helles is more bready, more sweet and has more body than a pilsner.

Kölsch

This one's a Trojan horse. An ale in lager's clothing. It's a hybrid style that ferments like an ale but is cold conditioned like a lager. I've put kölsch with the lagers because it hits the same spot – smashable and satisfying. It pours pale gold, is beautifully clear, and tastes dry, clean, crisp and delicate. Thanks to the yeast, you may find it's also a little fruity.

Technically, a beer shouldn't be called a kölsch unless it was brewed in the city of Cologne (Köln) ... but I won't tell if you won't.

New world lager

Craft brewers love to take a traditional style, then tweak and modernise it with their own twist. For a new world lager, brewers take an older lager style and substitute the traditional hop varieties for bold, aromatic New World hops. If you want a pilsner with an extra hit of citrus, or a helles that uses New Zealand hops to add tropical notes into the mix, this kind of lager is for you.

IPL (India Pale Lager)

If a new world lager is a traditional lager with some hop notes poking through, then an IPL is an IPA with some lager characteristics poking through.

An IPL shows off the loud personality of hops, just like an IPA. But IPLs have a much lighter feel in the mouth, with that clean, crisp feel of an easy-drinking lager.

Big flavour, big bitterness, and a lean body. Does this make it an IPA made with lager yeast, or a lager that's been hopped through the roof? Who cares. It's delicious.

'Lager'

What if a beer is simply labelled as a 'lager'?

If it's from a craft brewery, the brewer is using this familiar word to effectively say, 'This is an easy-drinking beer.' It could be a pilsner, a helles or a kölsch; it could be traditional or made with New World hops. If you're lucky, there'll be more information in the label description.

If the beer is from a macro brewery, I'd refer to it as a 'commercial lager'. This kind of beer came into existence over time, as brewers wanted to make beers that had the crisp refreshment of a pilsner but were even more approachable. They toned down the malt character, toned down the hop character, toned down the bitterness. To make the beer drier (which is more refreshing and allows people to drink more of it) and reduce the cost, they replaced some of the malt with cheaper adjuncts – in America, corn or rice; in Mexico, flaked maize; in Asia, rice; in Australia, cane sugar. The result is a dry, pale lager with high carbonation, a gentle bitterness and a neutral flavour profile, designed to be drunk as cold as possible so you can't really taste anything.

Breweries that make these beers do a great job of brewing them, and an even better job of selling them; over three-quarters of the beer on the planet is commercial lager. This is a product that large portions of the population want to drink.

But these beers are also the reason so many people can drink beer without knowing what hops and malt taste like.

Amber lagers and dark lagers

If you like malt flavours – bread and biscuits, toast and nuts, caramel and toffee, chocolate and coffee, dark fruits and dried fruits – then discovering dark lagers will change your life.

Darker lagers have been around for much longer than pale lagers, but unfortunately they don't get much attention outside of Germany. When pale lagers arrived on the scene in the 1800s, they went on to rule the market and spread all over the world while darker coloured lagers … didn't.

But I say bring on the darker colours! These beers exhibit a depth of flavour you can't get in a pale lager, while often still having an impossibly clean and crisp character to them. It's miraculous.

Unfortunately, like miracles, these styles can be hard to come by. But they're worth the hunt. Is there a bottle shop in your area that sells German beers? A German restaurant or German club? A craft brewery that specialises in traditional styles or makes limited release lagers? Are there Oktoberfest celebrations in your city?

Or there's always the option of going to Germany itself. Travel around and taste the specialties of each region. Drink the beers they've been brewing for hundreds of years.

The beat of the drum

Have you ever cooked on a fire?

It's hard to get it right – flames blast the heat directly onto whatever you're cooking and smoke gets into everything. If you're kilning malt with wood fire, you have all of these issues and end up with dark, smoky malt and dark, smoky beer.

In the early 1800s, a new kind of kiln was invented – a rotating drum that used hot air rather than the direct heat of a wood fire. This was a game changer for beer. Brewers had more control over the colour, flavour and consistency of their malt. Dark and smoky was still an option, but now lighter colours and nuanced flavours were options too.

This technology came to life in England, but a couple of sly brewers from Germany and Austria headed across the pond to learn this new way of malting and took the knowledge back to their breweries. They're the ones who invented the Märzen and the Vienna lager.

Some kinds of amber lager

Vienna lager

The colour of copper and the taste of toast. If you're after something as drinkable as a pale lager but with an injection of flavour and complexity, this is for you.

Märzen

Märzen was traditionally brewed in March ('Märzen' is German for 'March') and stored until Oktoberfest. It drinks like a slightly amped up version of a Vienna lager – more malty, more body, more booze. If Vienna lager is toast, Märzen is toast with a thin spread of golden syrup.

Bock

The traditional bock is sweet and strong – between 6% and 7% ABV – taking those toasty flavours mentioned above and adding a flick of caramel.

Want something stronger? Look to the doppelbock, which clocks in anywhere from 7% to around 12% ABV. It pours a darker colour and has flavours of chocolate and dark fruits peeking in, as well as the warming taste of alcohol. This one's chunky enough that monks drank it to supplement their diets. (Doppelbock also sounds like it could be a Dr Seuss character.)

Still not enough for you? An eisbock is a doppelbock that's been partially frozen and had the ice removed, leaving the remaining concentrated liquid stronger than the original. Will it be 9% ABV? 13% ABV? 35% ABV? This style is a moveable beast. Expect intense flavours like a chocolate-coated prune liqueur.

Rauchbier

Colour-wise this fits in with the amber lagers, but brace yourself for something different. Rauchbier literally means 'smoke beer', and that's what you're getting here – an amber lager made with smoked malt. Depending on the malt used, these beers can offer a gentle thread of maple-bacony smoke or a faceful of campfire smoke.

Some kinds of dark lager

Munich dunkel

If a beer is simply labelled 'dunkel', it's most likely a Munich-style dark lager. (The word 'dunkel' just means 'dark' so don't get this confused with, say, a dunkelweizen – dark wheat beer.)

A Munich dunkel tastes like toasted bread crusts, perhaps with some nuttiness or chocolate in there as well. Thanks to caramelised sugars in the darker malts, you may also get some light toffee or caramel notes. But don't expect anything too sweet. This brown lager is still crisp, and still begs to be drunk by the stein.

Schwarzbier

A dark beer with none of the heaviness people associate with stouts and porters. Schwarzbiers are darker than dunkels, but drier and lighter on the palate, making them surprisingly easy to quaff. You'll get those dark malt characters – smooth roast, rich bread with a hint of dark caramel, bitter chocolate – but they're quite gentle.

Schwarzbiers were the inspiration for Japanese black lagers, giving a dark (but still crisp) alternative to the usual pale rice lagers.

'Schwarz' means black, but if you hold a schwarzbier up to the light you'll see some dark brown and deep red. Personally, I prefer to keep it out of the light and pretend I'm drinking liquid obsidian.

Baltic porter

My first ever Baltic porter blew my mind. It flooded my palate with some of the best porter-like malt characters I'd had – chocolate and dark fruits and liqueur notes – but it had a smoothness unrivalled by porters or stouts.

Technically this lager can sit between 6.5% and 9.5% ABV, but I reckon a 6.5% Baltic porter is a waste of a Baltic porter. These babies shine when they're at the stronger end and they drink almost like a fine port served with soft liquorice or dark chocolate.

Pale ales

Pale ales have been around for hundreds of years in one form or another. But from the 1980s onward they changed the shape of beer forever, rescuing millions of beer drinkers from a prison of one-dimensional beer.

(They may also be the only kind of beer that rhymes. More research needed.)

Pale ales offer distinct character while still being approachable. Because of this, they're sometimes referred to as 'gateway beers', since they open people up to a world of beer styles and flavours.

But they're not just beery training wheels; you could drink pale ales your whole life and never get sick of them. The range of flavours is vast – brewers can switch up the ingredients just a little to change the flavour profile entirely. When you look at all the pale ales around – including the pale ales hiding behind labels like 'session ale', 'summer ale' and 'refreshing ale' – you realise no one could ever get to all of them. (Please don't try. Your liver won't cope.)

Pale in comparison

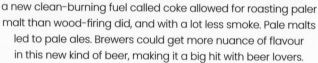

**In the lager section, we saw how
pale lagers were made possible in
the 18th century with the invention
of the drum kiln. For pale ales,
let's look back even earlier.**

Wood-firing malt was the norm in Britain, since
using coal as a fuel would put awful tasting
smoke into the grain. But in the 17th century,
a new clean-burning fuel called coke allowed for roasting paler
malt than wood-firing did, and with a lot less smoke. Pale malts
led to pale ales. Brewers could get more nuance of flavour
in this new kind of beer, making it a big hit with beer lovers.

These beers wouldn't be recognisable as pale ales by
modern standards. But technology keeps marching on
– from coke to the drum kiln to the work of biochemists
and microbiologists in the field of malting today.

As a simple guide, I think of English pale ales as malt-driven, American pale ales as hop-driven, and Belgian pale ales as yeast-driven. And that's helpful … to some extent. (Perhaps that should go on my headstone when I die: 'Here lies Mick Wüst. He was helpful … to some extent.')

But that's very simplistic. While pale ales share some common traits – they're easy to drink and refreshing, and mostly sit between 4% and 6% ABV – they're all delightfully different. The best thing to do is explore them for yourself.

It's hard to go wrong with a pale ale.

Some kinds of pale ale

English pale ale

Pale ales were invented in England, so it's only fair these get listed first.

Copper-hued English pales are proof that pale ales don't have to be the lightest colour possible; remember that pale ales were named in comparison to dark ales.

The colour in these beers is thanks to the use of crystal malts, which also lend caramel and toffee notes to the lighter biscuity or nutty malt character. But while malt is at the forefront, English hops bring a thread of floral, earthy or even woody flavours.

If a craft brewery makes a beer called an extra special bitter (ESB), it probably fits in here. But for bitters poured from the cask in an English pub, head to the section on other European beers.

American pale ale

While English pale ales are polite and mild-mannered, American pales are loud and in-your-face. When American brewers took on the English pale ale, they toned down the malt and amped up the bitterness and hop character. The *kind* of hop flavours changed from the floral, herbal and earthy notes of UK hops to the pine, resin, citrus and other fruit notes of American varieties. And the *amount* of hop character changed as American brewers loaded hops in for their punchy aromas and flavours, as opposed to the softer approach of English brewers.

American pale ales (APAs) have evolved since Sierra Nevada pioneered the style in 1981. You'll still find some that capture the pine and grapefruit and spice of classic US hop varieties Cascade, Centennial, Columbus and Chinook ... but you'll find many American pales tend towards fruitier flavours nowadays, like the brighter citrus, tropical fruit and stone fruit flavours of newer hop varieties. I could list some – like Citra, Simcoe, Amarillo, El Dorado and Mosaic – but there are so many more. They multiply like rabbits.

America is a big place, and some beers are labelled with a sub-style like 'west coast pale' or 'east coast pale'. But more often than not, they're just called 'pale ale'.

Australian pale ale

This style is laid-back, has a cheeky grin and is keen to be your mate.

Aussie pale ales use Australian hops and are brewed with the subtropical climate in mind. They're bursting with fruit notes from varieties like Ella, Vic Secret and Topaz, yet they're generally more easygoing than their American counterparts – less bitter and closer to 4% than 6% ABV. If it's a scorcher (that's 'hot day' to you non-Aussies), this style is perfect for knocking back a few and still keeping your head.

Pacific ales fit in here too, oozing vibrant passionfruit aromas from Galaxy hops and showing a soft cloudiness thanks to added wheat.

American wheat

In my mind, American wheat ales absolutely belong in the pale
ale category: pale to the eye, low in bitterness, easy on the alcohol
content, playful with the hop character and neutral in the yeast
department. They just contain a higher percentage of wheat than
many other pale ales.

Hazy pale ale

Drinking a hazy pale ale is like drinking tropical fruit juice …
except, you know, with booze in it.

They're hazy in appearance (thank you Captain Obvious),
often have wheat or oats in them to add to the mouthfeel and are
heavily dry-hopped for huge hop aromas with minimal bitterness.

(See a fuller description of 'hazy' in the IPA section.)

XPA

Unlike English and some American pale ales, you won't find XPAs
(extra pale ales) relying on crystal or caramel malt. These beers
are all about being extra pale – lighter colour, lighter in the body
and lighter malt taste.

The hoppiness in XPAs is approachable and fruity, with the
zing of citrus and zap of tropical fruits. The stripped back malt
profile can help the same amount of hops stand out more – like
streamlining the body of a sports car so the same amount of
engine power makes it go faster.

Belgian pale ale

Compared to other Belgian styles, the Belgian pale ale is young; compared to APAs, it's not so young, being created around 75 years earlier.

Compared to other Belgian styles, the Belgian pale ale has a restrained yeast character; compared to APAs, it has a noticeable yeast character, with fruity and spicy notes dancing among the toasty and sweet caramel flavours of the malt and the grassy, herbal or floral hop notes.

Lots of flavour. Lots of balance. Lots to love.

American amber/red ale

I couldn't figure out where else to put this, so I'm sneaking it in here.

These beers are wonderful. They're something like a cross between an English pale and an American pale. There's an abundance of sweet caramel and toffee malt presence, but the American hops sing their lively song of pine, citrus, berry or floral notes.

And then there's the colour. These beers can span from a rusty amber to a deep copper to a glorious ruby red; brewers have good fun selecting just the right malts to make these babies shine.

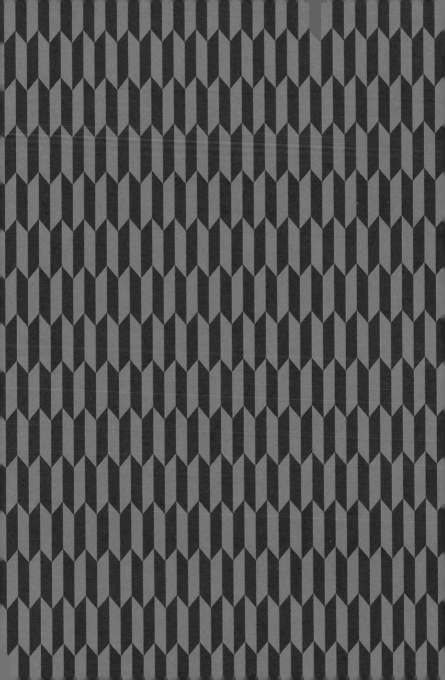

IPAs

While pale ales were the foot soldiers of the craft beer movement, India pale ales (IPAs) are the champions. They're now a mainstay of the beer scene, but have a bad habit of making people feel they need inside knowledge to decipher them.

They have a confusing name – the style didn't originate in India, and they're not all pale. And there are so many kinds of IPAs that it's easy to be caught off guard, receiving a bitter bomb when you were expecting a juice box or vice versa.

But a little knowledge goes a long way.

Where did the name come from?

In the early 1700s, British beers started being sent to India.

The myth: the beer sent to India was spoiling on the long sea voyage, so brewers loaded it with extra hops to preserve their product. In the process, they invented a new style – the bitter and hoppy India pale ale.

The reality: all kinds of beers were sent to India. But while dark beers were popular in England, it was the more refreshing pale ales that took off in subtropical India. The term 'India pale ale' started being used back in England as a way to hype up and sell more pale ales on home soil, and this marketing move began the slow evolution of a style.

There are IPAs in just about every colour, flavour and alcohol strength possible. Trying to define the category can be like trying to pick up a live eel with chopsticks.

But to boil it down to three things most IPAs have in common: they contain more hops (and hop character) than pale ales; they're more bitter than pale ales; they're higher in alcohol than pale ales, usually between 5.5% and 7.5% ABV.

As IPAs made their resurgence in America from the 1980s into the early 2000s, the above three traits were a given. IPAs were also all clear, like most lagers and pale ales.

But through the 2010s things became less clear – both metaphorically and literally. A new kind of IPA arose in America's New England region. Brewers started focusing less on the bitter acids in hops and more on the aromatic oils. They left hop particles in their IPAs for the sake of flavour instead of getting rid of them for the sake of appearance. The resulting IPAs were hazy and juicy, with low bitterness thanks to heavy dry-hopping.

These beers took off with gusto and spread around the world – the haze craze. They gained momentum and began to influence all kinds of IPAs (and pale ales): dry-hopping became the norm, hazy and juicy became common characteristics in hoppy beers, and bitterness decreased across the board. IPAs transitioned from the bitter gatekeeper of craft beer to the friendly face that welcomed people in.

Nowadays, any attempt to come up with a catch-all definition for IPAs ends up fairly blurry. But you can still expect the hops to do most of the talking in any IPA, whether that's with biting bitterness or gentle juiciness.

What's dry-hopping?

Dry-hopping is when brewers add hops to beer *after* the boil, usually in the fermenter.

This maximises hop flavour and aroma, since the delicate oils don't get cooked off – kind of like adding fresh basil after the pasta sauce has finished cooking. And since the bitter acids in hops don't dissolve in beer unless they're heated, dry-hopping can add plenty more hop character without adding plenty more bitterness.

Some kinds of IPA

English IPA

These are the big brother of English pale ales. A boost in hops brings a boost in bitterness, as well as aromas and flavours of English hop varieties – floral, spice, earthy, nutty. British malts stand tall with toffee, biscuit and caramel notes, making these beers more malt-forward than American IPAs.

Overall, English IPAs are designed to be balanced brews. It's American IPAs that really shine the spotlight on hops …

West coast IPA

Big and bitter. This was the most popular style of IPA during the rise of craft beer.

West coast IPAs (WCIPAs) are hefty beasts, often sitting around 7% ABV. Classic US hop varieties like Cascade, Columbus, Chinook and Centennial are loaded in to give bitter citrus, pine and dank notes. As varieties like Citra and Mosaic became popular in the 2010s, some WCIPAs showed more fruity notes.

While they originally had the chewy malt of English IPAs, over time WCIPAs became known for being dry, which intentionally threw them out of balance to let the hops dominate.

When IPAs with low bitterness grew in popularity, even west coasts softened up a bit. But a brewer who's nostalgic for the good ol' days may still make a palate-wrecking WCIPA.

Hazy IPA

Hazy IPAs are more approachable than west coast IPAs. Copious dry-hopping gives these beers huge hop aroma and flavour without the accompanying big bitterness.

Hazies tend to use fruit-forward hop varieties and yeast strains known for tropical fruit character, resulting in beers best described as juicy. They often capture a mix of fruit flavours like a bottle of breakfast juice. The use of wheat or oats gives a soft mouthfeel, pushing the resemblance even further.

Hazy IPAs have had more names than Jason Bourne including Vermont IPAs, east coast IPAs and New England IPAs (NEIPAs).

Red IPA

One of my favourite styles of beer.

Think of a west coast IPA with its malt dial turned up. The addition of darker malts brings deeper, richer flavours; smooth malty notes of caramel or toffee or dried fruit join the punchy character and bitterness of the hops.

And the colour! These could be a rusty gold, vibrant like blood orange marmalade or deep and brooding like a glass of shiraz.

Red IPAs remain wonderful even when they're not at their freshest – instead of deteriorating, these liquid rubies simply change. The malt takes on a stronger presence while the hops slip into the background, leaving their bitterness to balance the malt's sweetness.

American red ales are similar, but with a lower alcohol content.

Black IPA

Hang on … how can an India *pale* ale be *black*?

It's oxymoronic, but the use of dark malts in an IPA gives birth to these creatures of darkness. Never underestimate a black IPA – they roar with stout-like roastiness and espresso bitterness while potent hops throw their weight around with citrus peel or resin and teeth-clenching bitterness. There are black IPAs that could be called smooth or subtle … but they're rare.

They can also be called India black ales or Cascadian dark ales.

Double IPA and triple IPA

Double IPAs – aka DIPAs, imperial IPAs or IIPAs – sit up in the area of 8% to 10% ABV. The main attraction is the stronger flavours: there's the taste of the alcohol itself; there's the extra malt used to boost the alcohol content, which usually means more residual sugars; and then this begs for more hops to restore balance. DIPAs are beers to blow you away.

Triple IPAs – or IIIPAs – are another step up. At 10% to 12% ABV, these can be rocket fuel if not handled well. But in the hands of a skilled brewer, they'll be delightful sippers that drink like a hoppy liqueur.

Occasionally you'll see a IIIIPA or a IIIIIPA. At this point there are no rules, and brewers are just playing with names. And with people's lives.

Rye IPA

The use of rye malt in an IPA lends a peppery or spicy character, which either complements spicy hops or contrasts with fruitier hops. Rye can also give a dry mouthfeel, so the bitterness cuts through more.

Belgian IPA

Outside of Belgium, this will usually just be an IPA made with Belgian yeast strain – mix the intensity of an IPA with the complex fruit and spice characters of banana bread or fruitcake.

A Belgian IPA by a Belgian brewer is more likely to be Belgian pale ale, tripel or golden strong ale that's been loaded with extra hops.

Session IPA

An IPA that's down in the zone of 3.5% to 5% ABV. Many brewers will debate the very existence of session IPAs ('It's just a hoppy pale ale!'), but the category seems to have stuck around.

Brown ales, porters and stouts

When I was a teenager, I tried my first stout. It was like licking a half-smoked cigar that had been flicked onto the ground and walked over by many feet. But just as the bitterness of IPAs is an acquired taste, so are the complex flavours of dark beers. In my early 20s, as I started acquiring a taste for dark chocolate, coffee and whisky, I fell in love with dark beer. And trust me – there's a lot to love.

Brown ales, porters and stouts still contain plenty of pale malt, but their distinctive colours and flavours come from the addition of darker malts. I think of them as three overlapping styles along a spectrum rather than entirely separate styles, increasing in flavour intensity as they slide up the spectrum. But there are plenty of exceptions, so take this with a grain of salt.

If it's not already clear from the previous style sections, sometimes a beer is labelled with a place name – like 'Belgian pale ale' or 'west coast IPA' – and it's a comment on the *style* of beer rather than where this particular beer was brewed.

While brown ales, porters and stouts are originally English styles, your English porter could be made by an English brewer or an American brewer. Or an Australian living in Japan could make an American stout. And for some extra fun, when we get to Russian imperial stouts ... they originated in England, not Russia.

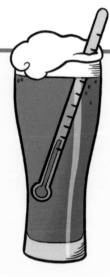

Lay your hands on me

Dark beers aren't meant to be drunk as cold as possible; their flavours sing when they're between 7°C and 12°C. But you don't need to be that guy whipping out a tiny thermometer at the pub (I assume these people exist). Just wrap your hands around the glass for a couple of minutes – your body temp will bring the beer up a few degrees, and it'll be good to go.

Some kinds of dark beer

Brown ale

Brown ales are the ideal dark beer to drink during the day. They're relatively light and refreshing, but full of malty goodness – biscuit, toast, nuts, brown sugar, caramel, toffee or even some light chocolate notes sneaking in.

There are brown ales with nuts or nut essence added to them. They're things of beauty.

Beers labelled 'dark ale' probably sit at the milder end of this category, while American browns sit around the 5% or 6% mark and are hoppier than their English counterparts.

Porter

Porters are named for the working-class cargo carriers in 1700s London who loved this kind of beer. But don't go thinking there's anything uncultured about porters. They taste like smooth jazz saxophone in liquid form.

They tend to lean into milk chocolate notes, but hints of coffee can start to creep in like a sip of cappuccino. Brewers will sometimes add cocoa, cacao nibs or chocolate to make a chocolate porter, and we love them for it.

An English-style porter will be all about nuanced malt and sit between 4% and 6% ABV, while an American-style porter will have a hoppy thump and higher ABV oomph.

Stout

While brown ales and porters will allow some reddish light to shine through, stouts are often black and opaque. To paraphrase Nietzsche: if you stare into the stout, the stout stares back at you.

The flavours of stout can punch a little harder than brown ales and porters. As well as chocolate and caramel notes, you can find flavours that'll rough you up a bit. A jolt of espresso. A stab of black liquorice. A shudder of roastiness (that bitter flavour in roasted coffee and dark toast). Stouts may be an acquired taste, but they're addictive when you enjoy them.

An oatmeal stout is fuller bodied and smoother than a regular stout (and doesn't taste like oatmeal).

A milk stout contains lactose, which adds sweetness, balances bitterness, and gives a silkier feel on the tongue. Tasty as is, or with additions like vanilla, coffee or chocolate.

You know the drill with American styles by now – an American stout will have more booze and won't skimp on the hops. Think of it like a black IPA trying to keep its voice down.

Imperial stout

Finally – FINALLY – we've arrived at my favourite style. I could write Shakespearian sonnets about imperial stouts. (What rhymes with 'orgasmic'?) But this book isn't called 'Suds & Sonnets', so I'll try not to break into verse.

In my not-so-humble opinion, the hearty oomph of stout flavours fits best with a burly alcohol content, and imperial stouts are about as burly as they come – they range from 8% ABV up to 18% ABV (though around 10% ABV is more common).

More booze comes from more malt, which usually also brings more sweetness and body too.

For all their heft, imperial stouts aren't just blunt weapons wielded by brewers to bash their drinkers into oblivion. Brewers work carefully with ingredients to take the flavours of a stout then balance the bitterness with sweetness, fill out the mouthfeel until it feels like you're drinking motor oil (in a good way), and add in some warming alcohol flavours. When the brewer has done their job properly, the result is something that sips almost like a dark beer liqueur.

Barrel-aged imperial stouts are a step up again. Any harsh alcohol flavours are smoothed out over months or years, and the liquid can take on some character from the oak and spirits that previously lived in the barrel. If you're ready for a beer that's shrouded in darkness, wearing a black cape and peering out of the midnight shadows (yes, I'm channelling Batman here), hunt down a bourbon barrel-aged imperial stout and welcome the night.

While you can drink imperial stouts fresh, they also hold up well with age if stored in good conditions; you can cellar them for up to a few years to allow the flavours to keep developing.

In case you were wondering about the name – 'imperial stout' is a shortened form of 'Russian imperial stout' (RIS), which was the name a London brewery gave to the strong stouts they sent to Czarina Catherine the Great in the 1700s. Ship these beers 2000 km and they're still fit for royalty.

What are barrel-aged beers?

Brewers can age strong beers in wooden barrels (usually oak) for months or years to add complexity to the flavours.

The very slow exposure to oxygen can round out flavours; the oak itself can impart flavours like vanilla, spice or coconut, as well as texture; and if the barrel recently housed a spirit like bourbon or rum, those flavours make their way into the beer as well.

It ain't cheap and it takes a long time. But barrel-aged beers are masterpieces.

Pastry stout

These decadent treats are designed to mimic desserts, pastries and other confectionery.

Rocky road stout? Peanut brittle stout? Salted caramel fudge brownie stout? Or perhaps you prefer Turkish delight or vanilla slice or s'mores or chai lattes or maple-glazed donuts …

Anything's up for grabs in this crazy Willy Wonka world.

Brewers get these flavours by loading these beers up with lactose and other ingredients – vanilla, chocolate, peanut butter, marshmallows and whatever else.

Pastry stouts are strong, they're thick, and they'll give you a sugar rush.

Sours

Sour beers can bring a kind of shocking refreshment on a hot day like dunking your head in cold water, and they can cut through greasy foods like nothing else. They're certainly not for everyone. But for people who like to bite into a wedge of lemon or touch electric fences to feel the zap ... sours are life.

Back in ye olde days, all beer was sour. You try brewing without stainless steel and modern refrigeration and see if you can do any better.

Over time, by trial and error, many brewers developed ways of keeping beer from going sour. Then when we developed a better understanding of microorganisms and food hygiene (thank you Louis Pasteur), the world of beer changed forever. Sour beer was largely a thing of the past.

But some kinds of beer remained intentionally sour, especially in Belgium and Germany. We're talking artfully crafted beers where different kinds of yeasts and bacteria create flavours that simply don't exist in non-sour beer. Some are light and refreshing, some are fruity and funky, some are characterful and complex. Some have a gentle tang of acidity, some are dry and tart and some are face-puckeringly sour.

When craft brewers discovered sour beer, they didn't hold back; they learned from the masters, played with traditional methods and experimented with new methods. And the sour renaissance began.

Microorganisms may be tiny, but they make all the difference in beer. For most beer styles, brewers want their specific yeast in there, and do their best to keep all other tiny beasts and bugs out. But in sour beers, brewers let a few of these other little beasties do their thing. These bacteria produce lactic acid, which is perfectly safe to drink and gives the beer a sour taste.

There are different ways to sour a beer. There's kettle souring, where the brewer adds specific strains of bacteria to get a controllable amount of acidity. There's mixed fermentation, where a brewer releases a zoo of tiny monsters into the beer to run rampant and give more complex acidity and flavours. And there's spontaneous fermentation, where brewers hand the reins over to wild yeast and bacteria – from the air, from fruit, from wooden barrels – and see where it takes them.

Say g'day to Brett

Brettanomyces (or Brett for short) is a type of wild yeast that can ferment sugars and produce flavour compounds, just as ale yeast and lager yeast can. It's long been the nemesis of winemakers, but brewers may choose to let Brett bring his bold personality to some of their brews.

Some kinds of sour beer

Berliner weisse

Berliner weisse is a sour German wheat beer with a long history – it's been around for over 400 years, enjoyed by emperors and workers alike. Traditional versions in Germany are pale, light in alcohol, lemony, bready and dry. But elsewhere, craft brewers often use them as the base for easy-drinking fruited sours.

Gose

Gose (pronounced goes-uh) is another sour wheat beer from Germany, but with a difference. Goses contain coriander seed and salt – juuuuust enough to hit your saliva glands and have you drooling for more. Between the dry tartness and the sea-breeze saltiness, this is a super refreshing style.

Lambic

Lambics have been made in Belgium for 800 years and get their unique flavours from the wild yeasts and bacteria of the Senne Valley. The brewers invite all these wild microorganisms in to party, then stick the beer in barrels for a couple of years. The flavour possibilities range from barnyard funk to cheesy, from wine-like to cider-like to who knows what else. It's crazy in there. It's like the cantina scene from *Star Wars*.

Flanders red and oud bruin (Flanders brown)

These Belgian sours may look and taste different, but Belgians consider them to be in the same family.

Brewers of Flanders red add specific yeast and bacteria to their brews, then barrel-age and blend to reach their desired goal – a reddish-brown beer with sour fruity notes (think cherries and plums) that remind you of an acidic red wine. It's hard to believe there's no fruit in there.

Oud bruin has some fruitiness, but the darker malts bring a range of different flavours too – think malty chocolate and caramel. Mix these with the sourness and this one is *not* reminiscent of red wine – or anything else, really.

Pastry sours

A world apart from traditional, these beers are a recent novelty. They're high in alcohol and stuffed with lactose, vanilla and fruit. These beers could be designed to taste like anything from a sour blueberry smoothie to a lemon meringue cheesecake.

Wild ale

Modern wild ales take their inspiration from traditional sours like lambics, but all wild ales are different. I can't really tell you what to expect here. If this is an area you want to explore … good luck.

Other European beers

These beers don't have too much in common other than the fact that they originated on the same continent. The fact that I'm squishing together styles from Ireland, Scotland, England, Germany and Belgium is no comment on their significance. I wanted to include them but didn't know where else to put them.

If you're from one of these countries and you're offended, come find me and I'll buy you a beer.

English mild and bitter

With their light natural carbonation and full body from the British malts, these are smooth beers made with drinkability in mind.

This family of beers ranges from around 3% ABV to 6% ABV. The flavours are subtle and nuanced, but there's plenty going on: malty characters of bread and biscuit, toast and nuttiness, sometimes a touch of caramel or toffee; fruity flavours from the English yeast strains; light floral, spicy or earthy hop notes.

These styles are best as cask ales – walk into an English pub, order a pint of bitter and let the good times roll.

What are cask ales?

Unpasteurised, unfiltered and naturally carbonated in the same barrel they'll be served from, these are cask ales (or 'real ales').

They could be milds or bitters, pale ales or brown ales, but they all continue fermenting right up until shortly before they're served and enjoyed. These are living beers, soft and smooth, and full of character.

While bottled versions of real ale exist, these beers shine when they're served as originally intended: in a pub, from the cask, at cellar temperature (around 12°C), by the pint.

And yes, that generally means a British pub – you won't find many outside of the UK.

Barley wine

Barley wine (or in America, barleywine) isn't wine, and there are no grapes involved. These beers got their name from having an alcohol content closer to wine than to most beers – between around 8% and 12% ABV.

English barley wines – the original – are generally sweet and malt-driven. I've had barley wines that taste like caramel sauce, like orange marmalade and like sweet port wine … and always with a nice boozy warmth.

American barleywines, on the other hand, are hoppier and more bitter. Huge surprise!

Barley wines are beers to sip like an after-dinner liqueur, not to chug by the pint. Unless you have a death wish.

Scottish ales

In the good times and the bad, the history of Scotland and England have been intertwined. As a result, their beers share some similarities, too. Scottish ales sort of resemble milds and bitters, but often with less hop character and sweeter malt notes of caramel and toffee.

A wee heavy is one of my favourites – it's like a barley wine, but specifically focused on those toasty and caramelised malt flavours. A good wee heavy is like eating toffee and drinking whisky at the same time.

Irish stout and red ale

Irish stouts are lower in alcohol and drier than their English counterparts. They're often poured on nitro for a creamy texture that softens their roasty bitterness.

Irish red ales are subtle, smooth and extremely drinkable – less bitter and hoppy than English bitters, less caramelly than Scottish ales, and drier than both thanks to the inclusion of some roasted barley.

German wheat beers

Wheat beers or weiss (white) beers, are hugely popular in the beer paradise that is Germany. They're made with at least 50% wheat, but the distinctive banana and clove (and sometimes bubblegum) flavour comes primarily from the traditional yeast strains used.

A good weiss beer often tastes like a good banana bread – fluffy and light in the mouth like the inside of the loaf, with the rich sweetness of banana playing off the restrained intensity of clove and other baking spices.

Hefeweizens are unfiltered and cloudy; kristalweizens are filtered and crystal clear; dunkelweizens are dark with flavours of toasted bread and caramel.

And thanks to the proteins in the wheat, you can expect a wonderful fluffy head that gives you a foam moustache.

Witbier

Another wheat beer called 'white beer,' but this one is Belgian. Witbiers are cloudy with fluffy white foam like their German cousins, but the gentler fruity flavours from the Belgian yeast are paired with additions of dried orange peel and coriander seed. Tie all of this together with luxurious effervescence, and witbiers are somehow rounded and delicate and bright and zesty and spicy and soft and creamy – all at the same time.

Trappist ales and abbey ales

Not only are there monks still making beer in monasteries in Belgium, but their beers have a cult following, are drunk from glass goblets, and are known as some of the best beers in the world.

Men of the cloth ... more like men of the froth! Am I right? (Sigh. I'm sorry about that. It's been a long day.)

The Trappist breweries in Belgium have each developed beers unique to their own monastery, but there are some styles in common across the board.

Dubbels, tripels and quadrupels sound like different riffs on the same style, but they're quite different beers.

Dubbels are strong reddish-brown beers that are toasty and chocolatey first, raisiny and plummy second, spicy third, and they finish dry.

Tripels are pale and spicy and bubbly with a solid pop of bitterness. They're complex – fruity and floral and peppery – but surprisingly easy to drink considering they can reach up to 10% ABV.

Quads (or quadrupels) are even heavier in alcohol, full of rich caramel and toast maltiness, brown sugar sweetness and all the dried fruit flavours you can handle. There's enough spice to let you know this is a Belgian beer, and enough boozy warmth to let you know this'll knock you on your cassock. (Trappist monks actually wear cowls, not cassocks, but this sartorial pun works better with 'cassock'.)

Some Trappist breweries export their beers worldwide, while others can only be purchased at the monastery, making them rare and highly sought after. Other breweries make beers that imitate Trappist styles, but they're generally referred to as abbey ales.

Saison

Let's step away from the monastery and into the farmhouse. Saison has its origin in rural Belgium, where farmers would brew beer for the seasonal workers (*saisonniers*) they hired at harvest time.

Saisons have a lively carbonation that lifts the aromas and dances across the tongue, a distinctive spice and fruitiness from the saison yeast, and a crisp, dry finish. Some are heavier, some are lighter. Some are sour or funky, while others are clean and sweet. But they all share a certain *je ne sais quoi*.

The craft beer movement loves saisons, but I reckon they should be even more popular than they are – after all, these refreshing beers were designed for knock-off drinks after a hard day's work.

What are farmhouse beers?

'Farmhouse' is an umbrella term that describes a range of beer styles and brewing methods.

The name comes from the origins – beers brewed on a farm, for the farm. The brewer (probably the farmer or his wife) used the ingredients available to them, and every brewer would have their own recipe and their own methods. And though they didn't know it at the time, each location had its own ecosystem of yeast and bacteria that shaped the beer.

Today, the term 'farmhouse' is used to refer to the styles and the flavour profiles that came out of this tradition – even if a beer is brewed by a professional brewer with commercial brewing equipment. Farmhouse beers are a diverse bunch, but you can expect them to be yeast-forward, sometimes sour and funky, and always interesting.

Most popular farmhouse styles are from the Belgian and French traditions such as saison, bière de garde and grisette. Other farmhouse styles exist as well, such as the maltøls of Norway, the sahtis of Finland, and the kaimiškas of Lithuania. But to find them, you may need to travel through rural Europe knocking on the doors of farmhouses.

section three

There are no rules for how to drink beer. That's the opposite of what beer's for! I've been living in a world of rules all day – now I just wanna drink my damn beer and sing along to bad '80s songs. But if there are things that'll help me <u>enjoy beer even more?</u> I'm up for that.

Fresh is best

There's an old German proverb along the lines of, 'If you can't see the brewery, don't drink the beer.' In other words, only drink beer close to the source – as fresh as possible.

I wouldn't recommend taking that saying literally, since it'd rule out drinking beer in your favourite dive bar, on a sunny beach or sitting in your underwear on your couch at home. But the proverb is worth listening to – beer is at its best when fresh.

We're talking about taste here, not food safety. Beer doesn't spoil easily in the way that milk does – alcohol and hops are both preservatives, so a bottle of beer can sit for years and still be safe to drink. But when beer is fresh, it tastes the way the brewer intended it. Everyone prefers fresh fruit and vegetables to ones that have gone brown and soggy. Everyone prefers fresh bread, soft and warm from the oven, to bread that's gone old and stale. Beer freshness matters in the same way. Fresh beer smells better, tastes better, and feels more crisp and lively in your mouth. It has zip and zing.

For hoppy beers in particular (like pale ales and IPAs), the first four months or so after brewing will reward you with bolder aromas, brighter flavours and more subtleties. Even a fresh lager tastes best when it's fresh. Beers approaching the 12-month mark can taste quite different to how they were originally intended.

There are exceptions to the 'fresh is best' rule. While losing hop character is anathema for American IPAs, some less hop-forward styles aren't impacted as badly by age. Some sours, dark beers and strong beers will even benefit from a couple of years ageing in the cellar.

But for the most part, beer is best when fresh. It's that simple.

A few exceptions ...

Beer changes with age, and some kinds of beer improve like fine wine.

There's an art to ageing beer (in short: keep it in a dark, consistently cool place) as well as a limit (no more than three years is a good rule of thumb). But if you cellar these beers in the right conditions ...

Imperial stouts – any hop character fades, bitter roastiness mellows out and complex malt flavours come together.

Barley wines – the booziness smooths out, the sweetness intensifies and dried fruit characters shine.

Belgian strong ales – as well as easing the booziness and upping the dried fruit flavour, age can soften the spicy Belgian yeast character into vanilla, leather or tobacco notes.

Lambics – the acidity will ease up, allowing the nuances of flavour to emerge.

Smoked beers – intense smoke will mellow out, the beer will sweeten and the flavours can integrate to become more cigar-like.

The four horsemen of beer unfreshness

Oxygen

Good for breathing. Bad for beer. Brewers work hard to keep oxygen out of their finished beer, but even the tiny amounts that inevitably get into a bottle, can or keg will slowly affect the beer. Hop aromas and flavours fade, malt flavours become stale or overly sweet, and the beer can eventually come to taste like wet cardboard. Yummy.

Light

When ultraviolet light hits beer, some of the sensitive hop compounds break down. Over time, these compounds can give off a sulphury smell and taste, similar to a skunk's smell. This could be the result of a small amount of light for a long time (say, a bottle spending months under halogen lights) or a lot of light in a short time (say, half an hour in direct sunlight). Kegs and cans block out 100% of light. Coloured glass bottles keep out some light. Clear glass lets all the light in for a free-for-all.

Heat

Your high school science teacher probably taught you that heat speeds up chemical reactions. Both oxygen and light will do their damage more quickly when the beer is warm or hot.

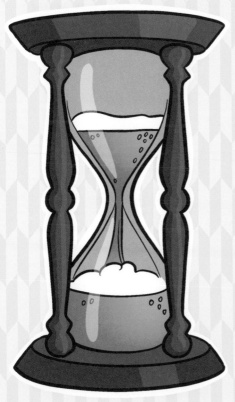

Time

While it's those first three horsemen doing the real dirty work, there's a reason we often talk about 'freshness' in regard to time. Some beers will keep their flavours for longer (such as higher alcohol beers, sour beers and malt-driven beers), but all beer will eventually deteriorate. Even small amounts of oxygen, light and heat will wreak their havoc in the end. Time is the great equaliser.

How to drink beer at its freshest

Buy it fresh. If a beer isn't fresh when you buy it, you have no chance of enjoying it at its best. Many beers will have a 'packaged on' date printed on the carton or on individual cans or bottles. Others only have a 'best before' date, which is harder to interpret since there's no standard rule for how long beer is at its best for. For many craft beers, the printed 'best before' date will be 9 months or 12 months after brewing.

If possible, take note of how the beer was stored before you buy it. Beer stored in the fridge or in a cool shop? Good. Beer sitting in the sun? Bad.

To protect your beer from oxygen and light, choose cans over bottles where possible – they keep oxygen out better than glass bottles do, and they keep light out entirely.

If you're drinking at a bar, you might have no idea when the beer was made or how it was stored. But as a general rule, if the bar has a regularly rotating range of beers, it's the kind of venue that cares about fresh beer.

Keep it fresh. You can't control how beer was treated before you buy it. But once it's in your possession, it's up to you, captain.

Keep your beer in the fridge if possible; otherwise find a cool, dark place. For most of us, the coolest cupboard in the house is our best bet. If you have a cellar, you're laughing.

There's only one time your beer should be in direct sunlight – when you're halfway through drinking it in the sunshine!

Drink it fresh. Want to enjoy beer at its best? Drink it sooner rather than later. It ain't getting any fresher.

Remember, think of beer like bread – best when fresh. Don't hoard it or save that one delicious beer for months for a special occasion. Just enjoy it. There'll always be more beer.

If you want something to save for a special occasion, get an imperial stout or a barley wine. Or a bottle of whisky.

Or … drink at the source. At the end of the day, you can always go back and follow the Germans' advice: beer is best drunk in the shadow of the brewery. Or, you know, in the sunny beer garden.

We're living in a golden age of beer, where breweries are plentiful and most local breweries serve up their beers on tap. This is about as fresh as it gets. You can't beat drinking a beer while looking at the tanks where it was made.

Serving up your beer

You know what I hate? When a brewer makes an excellent beer and packages it, but somewhere between there and my mouth someone makes stupid decisions that mean I get a less than ideal experience of that beer. Thanks to some thoughtless person's lack of care, I don't get to appreciate the beer as it was intended.

You know what I hate the most? When that person is me, and I have no one to blame but myself.

We talked about how important it is to store beer correctly to keep it tasting at its best. Now we're at the point of actually serving the beer up, and a few tips and tricks can make all the difference.

Some beer connoisseurs will insist on the exact right temperature for each beer, the perfect glass for every beer style, and a pour that takes several minutes and looks like you're measuring out dangerous chemicals in a laboratory.

I'm not that fussy. Sure, being pedantic about those things may technically give a slight improvement, but it makes my whole beer experience tedious and less fun. I prefer things to be quick and easy, so I'm happy to enjoy 80% of the benefit for 20% of the effort by just being a little intentional about how I serve up my beer.

If you're at a brewery taproom, bar or pub, you won't be the one making these decisions. But if you've got your hands on a can or bottle of well-crafted beer, it's been treated well up to this point and you're ready to drink it, then it's up to you now. If you want to experience the nuances and delights this beer has to offer, just as the brewer intended – and as the beer deserves – there are a few things you can do.

Let's treat this beer like the rockstar it is.

Why should I pour beer into a glass?

We've all got excellent memories of hanging out with friends on a summer day, drinking beer straight from the can. But pouring a beer out into a glass is the easiest, single best thing you can do to make sure you're getting the fullest experience of that beer as the brewer intended.

Appearance – pouring your beer into a glass both reveals exactly what colour the liquid is and forms the marvellous head.

Aroma – bottles and cans only have tiny openings, which barely let any aroma out. And besides, your mouth covers them entirely when you drink. Pouring a beer gives your nose the chance to enjoy the beer, not just because of the wider opening of the glass, but because the head that forms releases those aromas into the air for you to smell.

Taste – since most of the flavour we experience is shaped by our sense of smell, the flavours are much fuller and more nuanced now that the aromas are free. Why wouldn't you want to maximise the flavour of your beer?

Mouthfeel – when you drink straight from a bottle or can, an excess of carbon dioxide erupts in your mouth in a foamy reaction, taking over aggressively. When you pour into a glass first, you get to sip beer with the right level of carbonation, so you can appreciate the body and texture as you're meant to.

Another reason to pour

The beer in the bottle or can is full of dissolved CO_2. As soon as it gets the chance, that CO_2 will escape the liquid by forming into bubbles; this is called 'nucleation' (you'll see why that's important in a couple of pages).

When you pour a glass of beer, you see this foamy reaction as it happens, and it forms a head on top of your beer – where it belongs. You know where that frothy reaction doesn't belong? In your stomach.

When you drink straight from a bottle or can, you cover the tiny opening with your mouth and pour the CO_2-filled beer into your mouth and straight down your throat. And the whole way down, those thousands of bubbles are escaping from the liquid like passengers trying to flee the *Titanic*.

Welcome to Belchtown. Next stop: Bloatsville.

Whenever someone blames beer for making them gassy, I ask if they poured the beer into a glass first. Because if they didn't, then it's not the beer's fault – it's because they caused a chemical reaction in their stomach instead of pouring the beer into a glass.

So ... can I ever drink from the can?

Pouring a beer into a glass gives you a better experience of the beverage itself. The beer is objectively better this way.

But of course there are other reasons for drinking out of a can (or bottle) at times. You're out on the boat with a few friends, a clear sky and a slab of tinnies on ice. You're camping. You're in the pool. You're at a mate's summer barbecue, flipping burgers and crushing cans.

Drinking straight from a tinnie that's been sitting in ice for hours breaks all the rules ... but if you're anything like me, some of your best memories come from these times.

So by all means, go for it. You don't always have to make the most of the beer – as long as the beer's helping you make the most of the moment.

Pay attention to the temperature

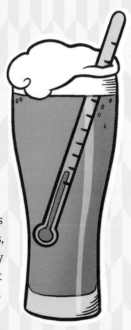

No one wants warm beer. I think it's safe to assume we already all agree on this. If you want warm beer, you're a barbarian.

But being too cold is also a problem for beer. Aromas are made up of lots of tiny particles in the air, and you want those particles to get into your nose. When a beer's too cold those particles sit still in the glass, huddling up and refusing to budge. And very coldbeernumbsyourtastebuds,too.Thismight be fine for bland commercial lagers, but it's not ideal for a flavoursome beer!

Most refrigerators are set between 1°C and 3°C to keep your food fresh. This is fine for storing beer in, but you don't want to drink good beer at that temperature – you want it a bit warmer to show off its aromas and flavours.

There are two simple ways to bring your beer up to a better drinking temperature: to warm it up a little/slowly, take it out of the fridge and wait – the room temperature will do the work; to warm it up more/quickly, wrap your hands around it – your body heat will do the work.

Different kinds of beer benefit from different temperatures, depending on what that style is emphasising: pale lagers are less about highlighting aromas and more about cool refreshment, whereas you want your IPA to be highly aromatic and a little refreshing. And a fine imperial stout is all about nuance, and not for chugging to cool you down after mowing the lawn. This isn't a hard and fast rule, but if in doubt: the darker the beer, the higher the ideal serving temperature.

Here's a guide for different styles:

- **Bland or bad beer** – as cold as possible. Numb those tastebuds.

- **Pale lagers and pale ales** – 3–7°C. Take it out of the fridge a few minutes before you're ready to open it. Try not to hold it in your hands while you're not drinking it, so it stays colder for longer.

Ambers and reds, IPAs – 4–10°C. Take it out of the fridge a few minutes early, then don't be afraid to hold it in your hands as you drink.

Dark beers, strong ales – 7–13°C. Take it out of the fridge several minutes before you're ready to open it, and cup it in your hands while you drink.

Imperial stouts, barley wines, strong ales, quads – 10–14°C. This is approximately 'cellar temperature'. Take it out of the fridge several minutes before you're ready to open it, and nurse that beer between your hands like it's a baby bird. If you're weird like me, you might even clamp it between your thighs for a bit. (Never do this to a baby bird, though.) Hold it in your hands while you drink.

Sour beers – dealer's choice. Want to dial down the acid? Drink it cooler. Want to dial up the fruity nuances? Warm it up a bit.

Remember, the temperature of your beer will keep changing after you open it. It's an opportunity to appreciate how the aromas and nuances of flavour keep opening up as you drink.

Pay attention to the glass

Designer glassware is an impressive field. It's not just the aesthetics (though they are things of beauty); I'm always amazed by the attention to detail that goes into creating just the right shape of glass to emphasise the characteristics of each style of beer. Some shapes focus on head retention, while others have ridges to agitate the beer and create more foam as you drink; some focus on keeping the delicate hop aromas tight and focused just inside the lip of the glass, while others release it in a barrage; some are shaped to give the liquid a high surface area and allow you to swirl the beer and open up its nuances.

So: do different kinds of glasses influence your drinking experience? Absolutely.

Do you need to own a different glass for every single beer style? You do not. (Though if you like having options, have fun building your own collection!)

Let's look at a few different kinds of beer glasses, but then I'll let you in on my little secret …

Nonic pint glass

This shape wasn't designed to help drinkers experience beer differently, but to help bartenders – the bulge stops it from slipping out of your hand (fewer breakages), stops the glasses from forming a seal when you stack them (quicker to collect and wash), and protects the rim from getting chipped and nicked (the name comes from 'no-nick'). But it holds a lot of liquid, it's good for gulping down easy-drinking beers, and it makes you feel like you're at the pub.

Pilsner glass

A pilsner glass – or any other narrow fluted beer glass – is designed to show off flawless lagers in all their glory. The narrowness of the glass encourages a luscious head to form and stay put, and also allows light to shine through the beer easily (there's not as much liquid to pass through) to show off the beer's colour and clarity like a sparkling gemstone. It sacrifices aroma by having a low surface area for the liquid, but that's not a priority for most pale lagers.

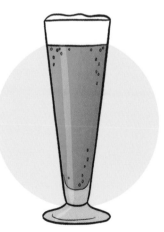

Wheat glass

German brewers pride themselves on the attractive fluffy head on their wheat beers, so it makes sense there'd be glasses designed to highlight this. Those sexy curves are there to promote a thick head within the glass, and also allow the foam to rise up above the top without spilling.

Snifter

These look like you should be drinking brandy out of them. They're designed for fancy beers with high alcohol – those imperial stouts and barley wines you've been saving to share with a friend. The shape begs for you to hold the bowl in the palm of your hand to warm your drink up a few degrees. You often only have around 200 ml of liquid in the glass, so there's plenty of room to swirl the beer to stir up those complex aromas. Classy. Then stick your nose in there for a good sniff.

IPA glass/stout glass

If a beer is crammed full of aromatic hops or specialty malts, why not get the most from it from first to last sip?

The narrower top of these glasses makes for a nice head when the glass is full. When you're halfway down, there's a wider section – swirl your beer to get that foam going and get the aromas pumping again. Near the bottom, there's a ridge or ridges to agitate the beer, maximising aroma and flavour from those last few mouthfuls.

Belgian beer goblet/chalice

These are things of beauty. They're wide mouthed bowls on a stem, sometimes slightly tapered in towards the top. Many Belgian breweries, including Trappist breweries, have a unique glass with their brand printed on it. Some of them even have some gilt edging. When you drink a sweet and spicy Belgian beer out of one of these, you feel like royalty. Talk about the holy grail of beer glasses!

Tulip

Now here's my little secret …
I only own one kind of beer
glass, and I couldn't be happier.
Don't tell the beer police. I own
a tulip glass (actually, I own four
of them for when I have friends
over), and it serves me well.
Honestly, I reckon it's the best
all-rounder beer glass. See if you
can figure out its benefits based on
all the glasses I've described above.

What if I have a favourite beer glass, but it's the wrong kind of glass?

Enjoy your favourite glass, that's what. And pity everyone who
doesn't have a favourite glass.

Survival tip

**What if you're staying in a hotel or you've
taken some nice beer to a friend's house
… and there are no beer glasses?**

Easy. Use wine glasses. Almost everyone has wine glasses,
and they're a great shape for a number of styles of beer.

Just make sure they're clean.

Pay attention to the pour

A well-poured beer not only looks fantastic, but it smells and tastes and feels better. You look at it and think, 'I'd pay good money for a beer like that at a bar!'

So remember: a well-poured beer is worth CASH.

- **C**lean glass
- **A**ngle the glass at 45°
- **S**low to begin with
- **H**ard towards the end

Clean glass

Make sure your glass is clean to begin with. Obviously you don't want to taste anything greasy or any residual detergent in your beer (gross). But on top of this, any dust or detergent in the glass will mess with the way bubbles form in your beer and affect head retention.

So even if it looks clean, it doesn't hurt to give your glass a quick rinse with water to get rid of any dust or detergent that might be hiding in there.

Angle the glass at 45°

When it's time to pour, start with your glass tipped at a 45° angle.

From the top of the glass to the bottom is a long way for beer to fall; if you pour it into an upright glass, the foam will get way too excited too quickly. Premature nucleation can be a real problem for some people. (That joke is literally the only reason I explained the word 'nucleation' earlier. Thanks for bearing with me.)

So as the pourer, you want to control how much foam there will be and when it will form. Tilting the glass means the beer won't have far to fall, which helps you start with a softer pour to minimise the foam at the beginning.

Slow to begin with

Start pouring slowly and gently. It's easier to make more foam soon than it is to undo a frothy mess. We've all seen a beer glass that's 90% full of foam. No one wants that.

The beer sliding slowly down the side of the angled glass should make minimal foam. Keep pouring like this until the glass is about half full to two-thirds full.

Hard towards the end

Now's the time to form the head by pouring hard. Straighten the glass up and pour the rest of the beer more vigorously into the middle. The beer should jump at the chance to foam up. Your aim is to get around one to two fingers of head.

If you make too much foam too quickly, it's not a big problem. You'll just have to wait for it to settle, then keep pouring when you can. This actually results in a great head, but it takes ages. Kind of a buzzkill.

A few notes ...

- **Don't chill your glass**; it makes for a bad pour and makes your beer too cold. And don't pour into a glass still hot from the dishwasher; a rinse with cold water should help get the temperature down.

- **If you're splitting a beer** into more than one glass, you don't have much to work with. Get that head going earlier.

- **Bottle-conditioned or can-conditioned** beers usually have some yeast sediment at the bottom of the container. It's not bad for you, but it can look a bit unappealing and make the last sip of your beer feel funny. Pour carefully and leave these dregs in the bottom of the can or bottle. (Don't stress if you accidentally pour it in. Just tell people you enjoy drinking your beer rustic-style.)

- **If you're pouring a nitro beer,** the rules all change – you're trying to make a big reaction. And you're probably going to make a mess, so do it on the kitchen bench or in the sink. Shake the beer a few times before opening, then crack it open and pour hard into a vertical glass all the way. Enjoy the show.

Engaging all five senses

Let me introduce you to a way I enjoy drinking beer – the five senses approach. A way of 'tasting' beer that engages not just your sense of taste but all of your senses.

Have you ever just stood quietly and listened to the world around you? It's surprising the number of things you hear that you hadn't noticed were part of the soundscape – birdsong, distant sirens, a refrigerator humming.

If you give your full attention to a beer with each of your five senses, you'll pick up on things that would have escaped your notice otherwise – the glorious colours, the aromas wafting from the surface, the interplay between malt and hops and yeast in your mouth, the bite and the bitterness and the tang and the texture.

You don't need any special skills or experience – just the willingness to stop and notice.

Pour your beer into a glass and start paying attention ...

Look at your beer. Holding it up to the light may help. What colour is it? Is it clear or hazy? What's the head like?

Smell your beer. Get your schnoz right up close and take a nice, deep breath in through your nostrils. If you can't smell much or if there isn't much head, try swirling and agitating the beer in the glass and trying again. What can you smell? Malty aromas? Hoppy aromas? Yeasty aromas?

Taste your beer. Have your first sip and notice if the flavours match up with what you were smelling or if different notes come through. What flavours are in the foreground? How about the background? How sweet is it? How bitter is it? Does the taste change from the beginning of the sip through to the end and into the aftertaste?

Feel your beer. Move the liquid around in your mouth. Does it feel thick or thin? Heavy or light? Textured or smooth? What does the carbonation feel like?

Listen to your beer. What stories is the beer telling you – about its ingredients, about how it was made, about the people who brewed it? What memories does it evoke? What does it remind you of? What emotions does it stir?

Pro tip

Say what you're experiencing out loud or write it down.

When you make yourself articulate what you're noticing, your brain does a better job of recognising what you experience. It'll help you remember, too, like repeating someone's name when you meet them.

I find this way of drinking to be an intensely satisfying experience. It's like a mindfulness exercise that helps you slow your brain, ground yourself in the moment and notice the good things in life. In this case, you're noticing good beer!

But this isn't just some beery form of navel-gazing. I'll show you some practical ways this can pay off in the real world.

Look

They say you eat with your eyes first. Is it so surprising that you drink with your eyes first? (Please don't literally drink beer with your eyes. That's an embarrassing visit to the doctor.)

What's the foam like?

One of the highest compliments my dad could ever pay someone is, 'He's got a good head on his shoulders.' And when a beer has a good head, that's worthy of a compliment as well. It's just so damn pretty.

On a lager, I love a majestic crown of white froth that threatens to stick in my moustache. But on a stout, I want a head that's as dark as the crema on an espresso and as thick as the foam on a barista-made hot chocolate.

What does the head on your beer look like? Is it soft and loose like bubbles in a bubble bath? Wispy and fluffy like a cloud? Dense like a marshmallow?

What colour is the beer?

I always marvel at the range of colours in the beer world. When I order a tasting paddle in a brewery's taproom, I love to choose beers from different places on the colour spectrum. One looks like merlot, another like pulpy orange juice, another like black coffee.

Hold a glass of beer up to the light to reveal its colour in full. What do you see?

Brewers and beer judges often talk about beer colour using the SRM scale (Standard Reference Method) of 1-40 or the EBC scale (European Brewery Convention) of 1-80. Both scales track from the palest beer (lowest number) to the darkest beer (highest number) and use standardised terms - Pale Straw, Straw, Pale Gold, Deep Gold, Pale Amber, Medium Amber, Deep Amber, Amber Brown, Brown, Ruby Brown, Deep Brown, Black.

These are helpful for brewers and judges ... but I'm a writer. I don't want to be limited by a short list of colours.

Play around with colour words. I'll gladly say a beer is glowing like an ember or shines with mahogany highlights or is pure obsidian. (Though maybe I wouldn't describe a beer as 'tangerine dream' or 'autumn whimsy' like they're paint swatches at the hardware store.)

Or if that's all too fluffy for you to whip out at the pub, you can compare your beer to other liquids.

Does this kölsch look like champagne - or more like sparkling apple juice?

Is this English bitter more of a copper colour or a rust colour?

Is this porter the colour of dark chocolate or motor oil?

Clarity vs haziness

For most of history, hazy beer has been the norm - styles like hefeweizens and lambics still show their natural haze.

But when you see a bright lager shining like a precious gem, you can understand why brewers often chase clarity in beer.

Bright beer is beautiful. Brewers will let their beer rest for a long time – or filter it – to get that that crystal clear look.

Clarity is the gold standard in lagers. It used to be the goal in pale ales and IPAs too, but since the 2010s there's been a huge movement in making beer hazy again.

Is the beer in front of you clear, hazy or somewhere in between? Does it look like sparkling apple juice, cloudy pear juice or opaque apricot nectar?

Does the beer leave lacing?

This one's for after you drink, not before. You'll sometimes notice a white residue left inside your glass as the level of beer goes down, spiderwebbing its way down the side of the glass as you drink. This is called 'lacing', and it can leave a lovely pattern for you by the time you've finished your beer. Who'd have thought even an empty glass could look good?

Admire your lacing … at least until you get another beer.

Smell

The aroma of beer isn't just an added bonus, but an important part of the flavour of beer. What our brains perceive as flavour is actually a mash-up of a few senses, with our sense of smell contributing between 75% and 95%.

This is why beer tastes better out of a glass – beer cans and bottles keep the aroma of a beer contained, while pouring a beer releases its beautiful aromatics. Drinking a beer without being able to smell it is like playing a game of pool with one arm tied behind your back – yes you can do it, but you're going to miss a few shots you would have got otherwise.

Once you've got a glass of beer, start with a gentle sniff from above the glass, but then get your nose right in there and inhale deeply. Don't be shy – you and the beer are good friends.

Some of the most common words people use to describe the aroma of a beer are 'malty', 'hoppy' and 'yeasty'. This is a good start. But nailing which ingredient is most prominent in this particular beer is just the first step. Those few ingredients can unleash a range of aromatics.

So let's channel our inner bloodhound and see if we can narrow in on what we're smelling ...

Malt aromas

Lighter malts smell like grain products. Does your beer smell bready? Is there a hint of water crackers or a whiff of sweet biscuits?

Toasted malts, caramel malts and crystal malts get more complex. Can you smell crunchy toast or nutty characters? How about sweeter notes of sticky toffee or sweet caramel or dried fruits like raisins or figs?

Darker malts bring deep, rich layers of flavour. Can you smell coffee? Is it more like a smooth cappuccino or an intense shot of espresso? Can you smell chocolate? Is it a light milk chocolate or a bittersweet dark chocolate? Can you smell burnt toast, tobacco, liquorice, molasses or stewed dark plums?

Then there's smoked malts that can have you smelling campfire, peated whisky, honey baked ham …

This is why the word 'malty' doesn't always cut it when we're describing a beer.

Hop aromas

There are hundreds of hop varieties with distinct traits, and their essential oils bring all kinds of aromatics to the table. Some people divide hop aromas into four quadrants – spice, floral, fruit and resin. It's a loose system, but it's not bad to launch from.

Spice notes are especially apparent in European hop varieties; we could include herbal, earthy and woody notes in here. Can you smell black pepper or star anise, black tea or freshly cut grass or cedar?

Floral notes are often subtle, but I find them to be calming like a bubble bath surrounded by scented candles. Can you smell lavender or rose (think Turkish delight) or musky perfume?

If you're like me, you may struggle to differentiate between the aromas of flowers and just stick with 'floral' most of the time.

Fruit notes are plentiful in our hop-crazy beer world, especially from American, Australian and New Zealand hop varieties. Can you smell citrus – grapefruit, orange zest or orange juice? Can you smell tropical fruits – mango, pineapple or passionfruit or some combination? How about berries, stone fruit or melon? Or even lemonade, blackcurrant cordial, raspberry candy or strawberry jam?

Resin includes aromas like tree sap, pine needles or incense. You may even notice a dank or weedy smell – since hops and cannabis are genetically related, they share some of those aromatic compounds.

Don't even get me started on the aromas coming from *neomexicanus* hop varieties: coconut and cream and vanilla and oak barrels full of bourbon …

Go home, *neomexicanus* – you're drunk.

Yeast aromas

In many beer styles, brewers aim to avoid specific yeast aromas and flavours, and they have the ingredients and technology to do this better than ever before. But that doesn't mean yeast aromas have disappeared from the beer world.

Can you smell juicy fruit notes in your hazy IPA? The yeast strain in that beer was chosen to complement the hops, boosting the aroma with notes of peach or mango or citrus.

Can you smell banana and clove in your German hefeweizen? People have been enjoying that aroma in German wheat beers for generations, and it's the yeast that deserves the credit.

Traditional Belgian ales are known for their distinctive yeast aromas. A saison can give citrus or stone fruit or black pepper notes or a Belgian pale ale might give a hint of strawberry bubblegum.

When wild yeasts enter the mix, the possibilities open up even wider. Different strains of *Brettanomyces* can bring all kinds of funky aromas to a beer: from light florals, through sweet pineapple or apricot notes, to savoury leather, barnyard or horse blanket.

It can be difficult to distinguish individual threads of aroma from each other.

The aromatics in a beer often blend together like different instruments in an orchestra, each bringing their notes and chords together to make harmonious music. Some people may be better at recognising sounds of the string section from the brass section, at following the bass line and the melody, at commenting on which particular woodwind instrument is their favourite. But we can all enjoy the music.

Feel

Mouthfeel. I feel like a pretentious snob whenever I say this word, but consider what a very simple word it is. Waterfall. Notebook. Mouthfeel. How does the beer physically *feel* in your *mouth*?

Brewers take mouthfeel very seriously. They pay attention to water chemistry and choose which grains will give more or less body to a beer.

For some styles they add unfermentable lactose to give a silky feel or add nitrogen for tiny bubbles that are oh-so-smooth on the tongue.

Mouthfeel shapes the way we drink and the way we perceive the aroma and flavour of a beer. When you're looking for maximum refreshment after a hard day's work, how good is a cold pint of crisp pilsner with a light body and lively carbonation? But when it comes to a post-dinner treat, I'd prefer the indulgence of a velvety stout that invites me to sip it slowly.

What's nitro

A nitro beer has a higher proportion of nitrogen than carbon dioxide. Since nitrogen has smaller bubbles than CO_2 and doesn't dissolve into beer as readily, it can bring a few differences ...

– Cascading appearance – when a nitro beer is poured into a glass, the bubbles all try to get to the top at once. It creates a cascading effect, like a million tiny helium balloons swirling around each other as they rise. It's mesmerising.

– Thicker head – the resulting head is gorgeously thick and dense like a marshmallow.

– Creamy mouthfeel – the beer feels thick and creamy as you drink it (though it can also go flat more quickly).

– Softer flavours – nitrogen dampens the way you perceive bitterness and acidity in beer, which smooths out the flavours. Some people like the softness; others say it mutes the flavours.

Some people love nitro. Some don't. It's worth at least trying for the experience – a treat for the eyes and the mouth!

Body

Would you describe it as light-bodied, medium-bodied or full-bodied? This is referring to the weight, density or thickness of the liquid. At one end of the spectrum, it could be thin like water; it can be light in the mouth like apple juice; a medium-bodied beer can feel more like orange juice or milk; or a truly thick and heavy beer might feel almost like olive oil.

You'll often find that beers low in alcohol have a lighter body that makes them easier to drink, while beers with a high ABV are more likely to have a fuller body since the brewer used more malt.

Bubbles

How's the carbonation? If the beer is more aggressively carbonated, the bubbles may feel prickly on your tongue or spritzy or lively. It's like they're having their own little party in your mouth, dancing on your tongue and releasing all those wonderful aromatics.

Or perhaps it's a softer carbonation, like when sherbet or champagne feels foamy in your mouth. A nitro beer will feel smooth and creamy, while a cask-conditioned ale or a barrel-aged beer may feel almost flat.

Crisp or clingy?

Does it feel crisp and dry? If the yeast was particularly voracious, there'll be fewer residual sugars in the beer to cling to your tongue. As well as giving the beer a lighter body, it can make the feeling of the beer disappear as soon as you've swallowed, like drops of water that sizzle and evaporate the instant they hit a hot pan. This is perfect in a sessionable beer (that is, a lower alcohol beer designed to be easy-drinking).

Or does it linger in the mouth more? More residual sugars can make a beer feel syrupy or chewy. It may feel like it's clinging to your gums or maybe it just leaves a tacky feeling on your tongue after you've swallowed, like paint that isn't quite dry.

Texture

Can you notice a certain texture? Some hazy IPAs are full of sediment to the point where they feel like pulpy orange juice, while fruited and oak-aged beers may pick up tannins that give beer a grippy feel on the tongue. Or maybe it feels entirely smooth.

All the feels

Then there are feelings that don't fit these categories. That tart, puckering feeling you get from a sour beer? The feel of hop oils coating your tongue as you sip a resinous west coast IPA? That whisky-warmth you get in your chest when you drink a boozy barley wine or Belgian quad?

It's nice to know there's a mouthfeel for every occasion, whether you want a spritzy smasher on a summer day or a meal-in-a-glass imperial stout that feels like you're drinking a brick wall.

Taste

The part where you put the beer in your mouth is the best part of drinking. Obviously. But hopefully by now it's clear there's more to beer than just the taste.

The reality is that taste – the actual sense of experiencing food and drink with your tastebuds – is limited to five basic tastes.

Sweet. Bitter. Sour. Salty. Umami. That's it.

I know what you're thinking: 'I can taste hundreds of different things!' But you're thinking of *flavour*. Our perception of flavour is more than just what we taste with our tastebuds. If you're up for a bit of food math (the best kind of math), you could say …

Flavour = taste + aroma + texture

So if you have a blocked nose and a numb mouth, your experience of taste will be quite limited (and kind of boring). But when you bring your senses of smell and feel to the party as well, you're going to have an excellent time exploring the wonderland of flavours available.

Beer and the five basic tastes

Sweetness. In most beers, sweetness is from malt sugars that didn't ferment. (In a few beer styles, unfermentable lactose is used to add sweetness.) As well as tasting different, sweeter beers will *feel* different, since sugars increase the body of a beer and cling to the tongue.

In beer, like in wine, the opposite of sweet is dry. Dryness is a lack of residual sugars – the result of the yeast eating up most or all of the sugars during fermentation. A dry beer will have a lack of sweetness, a crisper mouthfeel and less aftertaste.

So: does the beer taste sweet or dry?

Try to describe *how* sweet the beer is. A Munich helles might have a nice, full sweetness while an Australian lager is dry as a bone; a bitingly dry west coast IPA might catch you by surprise after a hazy IPA with a lingering sweetness; a pastry stout might be bordering on cloying while an Irish stout has a more-ish dryness.

Bitterness. In most beer styles, bitterness is a key part of the flavour profile.

It's also an acquired taste. As you taste more bitter food and drink, your tastebuds change so that you enjoy the complexity that bitterness brings. A beer you found overwhelmingly bitter a year ago can become your new favourite.

The bitterness in beer comes from acids in hops, and brewers measure the presence of these bittering compounds in IBUs (International Bitterness Units). Most beers sit between about 15 and 80 IBU, but they can range from 0–120+ IBU.

The roasted malts used in dark beers can taste bitter as well, like the bitterness of burnt toast or dark roasted coffee.

So: how bitter does your beer taste?

Does it have a soft bitterness or does it pummel your tastebuds with a bitter beating? Does the bitterness hit you right from the get-go or does it take a while to creep in, building with each sip then hanging around after you've finished?

How's the balance between bitterness and sweetness? Is the beer dry with an aggressive bitterness? Or does the sweetness carry the bitterness in its arms like a beloved pet or hide it entirely?

Do IBUs tell you how bitter a beer will taste?

Yes and no.

IBUs measure the amount of bittering compounds in a beer, so a higher number of IBUs will generally taste more bitter than a lower number.

But our perception of bitterness is affected by the other flavours in beer. Just like chocolatiers use sugar to balance the bitterness of cocoa, brewers balance the bitterness of hops with the sweetness of malt sugars. A dry pale lager with 20 IBUs may taste more bitter than a sweeter amber lager with 30 IBUs.

So while IBUs may help you predict how bitter a beer will be, take them with a grain of salt ... or, uh, sugar.

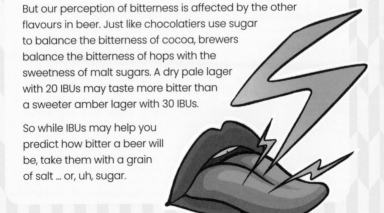

Sourness. Most styles of beer aren't supposed to be sour. (If you're served a beer that tastes sour when it isn't supposed to, you're entitled to politely send it back.) But there's a whole category of styles that are meant to be sour.

If you're new to sour beers you'll find the acidity distracting at first, which makes it hard to pick up other flavours. But over time, you'll start to notice the nuances: the red wine notes in a Flanders red, the citrus flavours in a lambic, the bready notes in a Berliner weisse. Or you can have easy fun with a mango sour or raspberry sour.

You can also grow an appreciation for the sourness or tartness itself. It's mostly lactic acid you're tasting (think tangy yoghurt), but some beers contain acetic acid (think vinegar) or citric acid (think lemon or sour sherbet).

Try to describe the kind of sourness. Is it more like a slightly tart apple or the sharp sourness of biting into a lemon? Is it a clean one-dimensional sourness or a complex sourness?

Saltiness. Unsurprisingly, you don't come across saltiness in beer very often. But if you find yourself drinking a gose – with or without added fruit – its gentle saltiness can be super refreshing and more-ish on a hot day.

Umami. Umami – or savoury – is not something you usually want in beer. Sometimes a stout can develop a taste of Vegemite or soy sauce with age. In small amounts, when there's the right balance of other flavours, this isn't a terrible thing. But if it becomes the dominant flavour, get rid of it. Who wants a Vegemite or soy sauce beer?

Exploring flavour

Malt, hops and yeast. See if you can distinguish any malt flavours. Start broad – bread, toffee, dried fruit? Then see if you can get more specific – wholemeal bread or brown toast? Raisins or figs?

See if you can distinguish any hop flavours. Start broad – citrus, tropical fruit, pine, floral? Then see if you can get more specific – grapefruit zest or orange juice? Pineapple or mango or passionfruit?

See if you can distinguish any yeast flavours – banana, pear, cloves?

Would you say this beer is more malt-forward, hop-forward or yeast-forward? Explore how the elements interact with each other. An American stout may have a strong coffee malt flavour with resiny hop character in the background; a farmhouse ale may be yeast-driven but with spicy hop notes around the edge; a hazy pale ale could be bursting with juicy hop flavours while slowly revealing a foundation of grain character.

Of course, if the beer contains other ingredients as well – fruit, spices, vanilla, coffee etc – then you've got even more elements to taste!

Boozy flavours. Are there any noticeable alcohol flavours? Particular in beers with higher alcohol content, you might get a booziness, a warmth, a liqueur-like taste. It may be well-balanced and smooth, like in a barrel-aged barley wine or imperial stout. Or it may be a bit rough, like a triple IPA that tastes as if it's been dosed with rocket fuel.

Low flavour vs full flavour. Not all beer is designed to have strong flavours. Pale lagers became world famous without ever overwhelming tastebuds. Clean, subtle, approachable, delicate, smooth, easy-drinking … these are all words used to describe beers that are low in flavour and high in refreshment. They don't grab your attention. You don't have to think about them too hard.

But other beers are full-flavoured and just beg to be marvelled at and talked about. Palate-wrecking bitterness. Rich chocolate. Explosive juiciness. Face-puckering sourness. These intense flavours make you say 'wow'.

When a beer is well-balanced its flavours tend to intertwine, so it's not always easy to dissect what you're tasting. And that's okay. To return to the orchestra metaphor: you don't have to pick out the notes that the second violin is playing in order to enjoy the symphony.

Don't overthink it. Just take your time and pay attention, and you'll train your palate. Chase down a beer flavour chart if you want some guidance in finding the right words.

And if you never get past 'sweet' and 'citrussy', who cares? As always, the main point is to enjoy your beer. If you're doing that, you're winning!

Listen

Okay, I'm cheating a bit with this one. It's not really about the sense of hearing. (I suppose you can hear bubbles popping if you hold a beer up to your ear. Do that at the pub and you'll also hear the scraping of chairs as people move far away from you.)

But you can listen to the stories a beer has to tell. Have a chat with the brewer or bartender. Read the label on the beer. Do a quick search on the internet to see what you can find.

What's the story of this beer?

'For this creamy fruited sour, the brewer added summer fruits to replicate his wife's favourite childhood ice cream.'

'For this Belgian-style table beer, the brewer used 80 kg of locally baked bread that was destined for landfill. It's a small contribution to reducing food waste, but had a larger impact on raising awareness of the issue.'

'For this wild ale, two brewers loaded a home brew kit onto a dinghy and took it down a river into the bushland. They brewed out there, with wild yeast and bacteria fermenting the beer to give it a unique, unrepeatable flavour. Talk about a beer having a sense of place!'

There are beers made with yeast from shipwrecks, beers designed to be enjoyed in space, beers fermented to the blast of heavy metal ... these are stories worth hearing!

What's the story of the ingredients?

'Did you know American Citra hops are so popular they outnumber the hops grown in any other country except Germany?'

'The malt, hops and yeast in this beer were all grown on the brewery's property.'

'Norwegian kveik yeast is amazing! It thrives at high temperatures that would kill other yeasts, ferments three times faster than other ale yeasts and is passed down through generations of families.'

What's the story of this style?

'When Napoleon and his troops moved into Berlin, they tried Berliner weisse and gave it the nickname 'Champagne of the North' because it's so lively and elegant.'

'Japanese brewers in the 1800s substituted out barley for rice as a way to sidestep some of the taxes on malt. In doing so, they made a new style of lager.'

'Bavarian brewers used to plant chestnut trees above their beer cellars to keep the ground cool and protect their beer. With the abundance of chestnut trees, they invented chestnut pilsners – and invented beer gardens, too!'

What's the story of this brewery?

I know a brewery that set up in a former World War II munitions factory, another brewery that uses traditional methods to make old world styles even when it takes longer, and another brewery that captures the whimsical excitement of a beer theme park.

I know a brewer who brings the technical curiosity of their engineering background, another who brings the experimental bent of their microbiology background, and another who brings efficiency from their time in the military.

What's the story of the artwork or the beer's name?

Beers wouldn't be half as fun if they all came in identical vessels. The decals and labels of beers can show minimalist design or anthropomorphic hops, psychedelic graffiti or gorgeous photos of landscapes, cute cartoons or cultural icons.

Then there's the names of different beers – a pop culture reference here, a hat tip to the style's origin there, poetic twists of imagination and puns aplenty.

What stories does this beer bring to my mind?

Sometimes the best stories are the ones we tell ourselves, and the ones we share with our friends.

'The first time I had a brown ale, my friends and I were sitting around a fire pit in the middle of winter, and it started to rain but we all refused to go inside …'

'Ever since I was little, my dad and I have made Christmas pudding together every year. He always gets one of these stouts, uses a bit in the pudding, then mixes the rest with lemonade to share with me ...'

'When I was in Europe, I went to this beautiful monastery on the outskirts of Prague that brews and serves their own beer ... and this hoppy lager makes me feel like I'm right back there.'

It doesn't have to be some deep-seated memory. Maybe the beer just gives you a vibe.

'I want to smash this zesty IPA and rock out to "Voodoo Child" on vinyl.'

'This barley wine makes me want to drink it in a leather armchair while smoking a pipe.'

Five senses in the real world

The five senses approach to beer can be as casual as you like. You're not filling out a dating profile for this beer, so it's fine if you don't mention every aspect. ('Did I mention foam and colour and clarity? Did it feel crisp or clingy? WAS IT CRISP OR CLINGY?!?!')

If I'm having a beer with a friend, it might sound something like this:

- **Look:** 'What a gorgeous cherry-red! It looks like stained glass. It's even coloured the head a little.'

- **Smell:** 'I can smell caramel, burnt orange, maybe some berries in there.'

- **Feel:** 'Ooh so thick and chewy! It feels like I'm drinking maple syrup.'

- **Taste:** 'That caramel tastes more like toffee now, with plenty of grapefruit peel. Quite sweet up front, but that bitterness sure sneaks up!'

- **Listen:** 'For some reason, this feels like drinking red cellophane. I mean, better than real red cellophane, obviously – I licked that once as a kid and it had a strange plastic taste. But this tastes like what I *imagined* red cellophane should taste like when I was a kid.'

The more you engage all your senses when you drink, the more you'll notice the differences between beers, from the obvious to the nuanced. You'll also get better at describing what you're looking for in a beer.

Being able to communicate these things can be helpful in a bottle shop or bar:

- 'I want a 6-pack of pale ale, but something bitter and piney rather than fruity.'

- 'Can you help me? I'm not from around here, but I want to take a selection of local beers home for my dad. And if you could tell me a little about the breweries, that'd be great.'

- 'What dark beers do you have? Nothing with lactose, though – I'm hoping for something drier.'

- 'I'm after something yeast-driven, maybe a Belgian, but nothing too spicy.'

- 'This raspberry saison … is it more of a subtle tartness or is it face-puckeringly sour?'

- 'Give me your haziest IPA. I'm talking completely opaque.'

The more you expand your repertoire and come to understand your own preferences, the more confident you'll be to branch out and discover new kinds of beer.

- **Like dark beer, but not sweet beer?** Try schwarzbier – or an Irish stout.

- **Like a full-bodied beer?** If a beer mentions lactose or oats or is high in alcohol, there's a good chance it'll be thicker.

- **Fallen in love with the intense flavours and boozy warmth of barley wine?** Check out some imperial stouts and Belgian strong ales for more malt monsters or try a triple IPA for a humungous hop bomb.

- **Like hop flavours, but want less bitterness?** Keep an eye out for 'hazy', 'juicy', 'NEIPA', 'double dry-hopped' or 'triple dry-hopped' – these all hint that a beer will be less bitter.

- **Enjoy simpler sour flavours?** Try a fruited kettle sour. Ready to try more adventurous sour flavours? Get your hands on a wild ale or a Belgian sour such as a Flanders red or a geuze.

The right beer at the right time

In a world that says have whatever you want whenever you want, I enjoy setting boundaries in the way I eat and drink. If I'm eating in an Italian restaurant, I'll make sure I order an Italian wine rather than a Spanish one. There are certain foods I'll only eat at Christmas even though they're available all year round, and while hot cross buns are on the shelves from January, I won't touch them until Good Friday. This gives me a sense of time and a sense of place and a sense of occasion; a sense of 'this just *fits* right'. It helps me make memories that are clearly distinct rather than all blending into one.

In the same way, I get a kick out of drinking certain beers at certain times. Sure, I could just always drink my favourite style, but there's something fun about matching the beer to the occasion. While booze has a bad reputation for making people forget things, drinking the right beer at the right time helps me to shape wonderful memories. I could describe to you the time I sat on a cliff overlooking the ocean drinking a west coast IPA with a resinous bite and eating my bodyweight in hot chips or that barrel-aged cherry imperial stout that I paired with chocolate Christmas pudding balls at my favourite bar. The beer makes the occasion better, and the occasion makes the beer better.

So here are some of my suggestions for drinking the right beer at the right time. If these ideas help you form some great memories – or even inspire you to create some occasions and traditions of your own – then I've done my job.

A style for every season

The fashion industry doesn't have a monopoly on changing things up every three months. Certain kinds of beer are just begging to serve your tastebuds as the weather shifts.

Summer

The days are long. The sun is out. The sweat is flowing freely. (It is in Brisbane, at least.)

When you're hot, drink a pale lager. You don't need to overthink it; when your brain is melting in the heat, you don't want to wrestle with decisions or complex tasting notes. An easygoing pilsner or a crisp kölsch will do the trick. This is when those beer ads from the '80s make so much sense – cold and refreshing are the main things you're looking for in a beer right now.

After your first one, if your core temperature has dropped enough that you can think clearly and you're ready for some hop character to chime in, hit the pale ales. The lower alcohol ones (perhaps below 4.5% ABV) will serve you well here; perhaps some lean XPAs or Australian pale ales.

One more thing: goses are underrated. It's not always easy to get your hands on them, but if you can, they work wonders. The tartness is invigorating, and the touch of salt makes them incredibly more-ish – and can maybe even replace some of those salts you've lost from all your sweating.

Autumn

The laziness of summer is well and truly forgotten. The temperature's beginning to drop. The leaves are changing colour. (Well, not on the trees where I live, but I like to imagine.)

This transitional season is the time to start transitioning into beers with more malt character. Let the colour guide you – amber ales and amber lagers will start to bring toast and biscuit notes, while red ales and red IPAs are likely to lead you into stickier caramel and toffee territory.

After enjoying lighter beers all summer, this is also a great time to dive into a few heavier and more complex beers. Imperial IPAs and barley wines and Belgian tripels go down a treat and offer interesting layers of flavour that the smaller beers just can't match.

Winter

There's a chill in the air. The sun is setting earlier. There's the temptation to curl up and sleep for three months.

The days are dark, and so should the beers be. There's no shortage of dark styles available: during the day, have a lighter-bodied brown ale or schwarzbier; as the afternoon ticks on, let tasty porters and dunkelweizens distract you from your shivering; at night, rug up with a warming Baltic porter or imperial stout.

If you're a hophead and simply can't ignore the pull of citrus and resin, a black IPA will stave off your withdrawals.

And if you're lucky enough to sit next to a roaring fire, find yourself a rauchbier – or any beer that has smoked or peated malt in it – and let the smoke infuse your very soul.

Spring

The weather's improving. The flowers are out. The birds are singing, and if the cartoons I watched as a child were telling the truth, there are baby animals everywhere.

It's a time to play around with flavours that give you a tingle. Fruited sours are just the thing for tantalising your taste buds, whether it's the gentle tang of a passionfruit sour or the acidic zap of a grapefruit sour. They can also bring a welcome splash of colour after months of wearing the same hoodie or overcoat day in, day out. A blueberry sour ale or a raspberry Berliner weisse always livens things right up.

Spring is a time of new life, so it's the perfect opportunity to taste all kinds of new things. Go to a bar and look for a style you've never tried before. Maybe it's a hefeweizen or an ESB or a Japanese black lager. Explore the Belgian section of an independent bottle shop and grab a kriek or a geuze. Maybe your local brewery has a lemon cheesecake beer on tap or there's a Polish restaurant serving all kinds of beers you can't pronounce. Let spring bring something new into your life.

A beer for every occasion

After mowing the lawn

A pale lager does the trick here (or after any kind of work in the sun). Ideally you want something without a strong malt sweetness. For bonus thematic points, find something with a bit of grassy hop character, like a German pils or a New Zealand pilsner.

Knocking off work

If you've been doing manual labour, go with a lager as above. But what if your work has you sitting down all day with your brain buzzing at a million miles an hour? Then you want something to help take your mind off it. Something to smack you around and make you stop thinking about deadlines and to-do lists and emails you haven't replied to. You want a bracingly bitter west coast IPA – the stronger the better.

Just come back from a run

When I'm halfway through a run, huffing and lumbering along with all the grace of a sweaty rhinoceros, I sometimes fantasise about the beer I'll drink when I finally get home. I dream of something light and dry, but definitely hop-forward and fruity – some kind of sessionable pale ale with a lean malt bill, like a melony summer ale or a citrussy XPA. The thought of it motivates me to press on and keep pumping those big rhinoceros thighs of mine.

Celebrating a special occasion

This is absolutely a time to share a barrel-aged beer with someone. Partly for the intense and complex flavours worthy of being sipped slowly, and partly because cracking open a barrel-aged beer adds its own sense of occasion. This beer has been waiting for you … possibly for years!

But don't overthink it. You don't have to invent a hover car or give birth to twins or discover a new species to be worthy of celebration. Next time an anniversary comes up or you change jobs or reach a fitness milestone, pop the top off a barrel-aged beauty and savour the moment with a friend or loved one.

At a picnic

Farmhouse ales are some of the most versatile beers to match with food. There's a whole host of flavours available within the category, with some beers managing to straddle fruity and sour and savoury and dry and refreshing all at once.

For my money, I'm getting a spritzy saison – delicate enough to enjoy before you've started eating, lively enough to cut through any of the heavier flavours, flavoursome enough to shine against all the bread you're stuffing into your face. (If your picnic isn't mostly bread-based, you're doing something wrong.) Bonus points if it's Belgian.

Tired, grumpy and just want the day to be over

In 1697, William Congreve wrote, 'Music has charms to soothe the savage breast.' I say a smooth brown ale or porter has the same charm.

Take it out of the fridge ten minutes before you're ready to drink it to let it warm up a few degrees. Pour yourself a glass, pair with some jazz, and before you know it your bad mood will start to lift. By the time you've finished your drink, you'll be feeling a little less savage and can slip into bed with a lighter heart.

At the beach

For this, you want a juicy pale ale that's just oozing tropical fruit aroma – the liquid equivalent of a Hawaiian shirt. (And it goes without saying, but forget the glass. You're definitely drinking straight from the tinnie.)

At the airport

Unfortunately, not many airports serve good beer. But you just need something interesting enough to chisel away at the drudgery of waiting; hopefully you can find an IPA or stout, and get yourself a $19 pint and a $34 bowl of chips to help keep the boredom in check.

On a dreary rainy day

Since this is hot chocolate weather, if you're having a beer, you want the closest thing you can get to a hot chocolate. That's definitely a chocolate porter – the fuller bodied, the better. Bonus points if it's on nitro.

With breakfast

Breakfast beers are a bad life decision ... but they're an excellent sometimes decision. A few times a year I'll have a beer with a hot breakfast and feel like royalty. My advice is that you want a beer that captures the vibe of whatever you'd normally drink with breakfast.

Orange juice drinker? Go for a citrussy hazy IPA. Coffee drinker? Find yourself a coffee stout. Tomato juice drinker? I don't understand you as a human. Please leave quietly.

Reading a book in a bar

This is one of life's great joys, and I feel I don't take advantage of it nearly often enough. Let me recline on a couch in a bar with an old paperback in one hand and a Russian imperial stout in the other hand, and I'm a blissfully happy man.

Bonus points if you're reading this book in a bar with a Russian imperial stout right now.

Christmas Day

I see people on social media opening their most exciting beers on Christmas Day – mixed culture wild ales, expensive barley wines they've been cellaring for years, dessert-themed pastry stouts – but honestly, I've never gone for a special beer on Christmas Day. I don't want to be distracted from the people I love, and I'm already stuffing myself with rich food. I want something easygoing to be the back-up singer rather than the headlining act. Give me a few malty lagers or clean pale ales, and I'm happy. There'll be plenty of other get-togethers over the holiday season where I can share my special beers with people.

A drop for every dish

Wine has always gotten attention as the drink that pairs with food. But there's more variety in beer than there is in wine, which means there are far more flavour combinations available to you by matching up beer styles with various dishes.

Brewers will sometimes let you know what foods go well with their various beers; there are beer and food pairing events where a brewer and a chef have worked together to create a scrumptious meal; and there are more recipes with beer in them than you can ever get to cooking.

I'm no chef, so I won't pretend to know all the ins-and-outs of flavour matching. But I'll share a few combinations my tastebuds never fail to thank me for ...

Pizza

Many would say a pale lager is the drink to have with pizza; if they're a real beer nut, they might push for a crisp and hoppy Italian pils.

But my go-to is a witbier. There's something about the way the zestiness cuts through the grease that I find delightful. Meanwhile, the light spice and creamy carbonation can make up for a bland pizza or be a fine accompaniment for a great one.

The exception is a pizza heavy with intense flavours. If you like to load up your pizza with double pepperoni or potent ingredients like olives or capers or anchovies or jalapeños or pesto, then slam that flavour bomb with a double IPA. I can't say you'll be ready to go for a run afterwards, but you'll have a bloody good time. Then you'll sleep like a bear in hibernation.

Fish and chips

When I was a kid, my family always spent our holidays at the beach. We'd sit down at a picnic table under the shade of Norfolk pines, looking over the golden sand and sparkling ocean, and eat fish and chips out of a paper parcel. To me, that's the taste of relaxation.

This is what I'm trying to recapture, so I want a piney IPA that's flavoursome enough to overpower the salt stinging my lips after I've been battered around by the waves.

But if you give me a Pacific ale with a hop profile that's as gentle as the sea breeze, I won't argue.

Another option is to get something lemony if that's what you like with your seafood, but this isn't always easy to find. Some lagers have a lemony flavour, brewers will sometimes release a lemon sour or you could hunt down a pale ale featuring Sorachi Ace, Southern Cross or Lemondrop hops.

Spicy curry

I've heard people say a strong-flavoured IPA goes well with curry, but I disagree. A good curry already has the perfect balance of spices and flavours. Why get in the way of that?

So I'll have a dry lager here to maximise the impact of the spices. It's perfect for scraping the tongue clean, leaving it ready for the next mouthful.

Note that this isn't going to help soothe your mouth if you're finding the curry a bit too hot; if anything, it'll make it worse!

Bread

I've already mentioned that Belgian saison goes well with bread at a picnic. But if I'm specifically thinking about the flavour of bread, I'm thinking about a helles. The bready malt taste is incredibly more-ish, and there's just enough body that you can imagine taking a bite of it.

A big hunk of fresh bread and a stein of helles; I'm in heaven just thinking about it. Or you can treat helles like it is bread, and match it with a platter of antipasto, cheese and meats or hummus and pickled vegetables ... with a bit of warm flatbread, just to be on the safe side.

(Is it obvious how in love with bread I am?)

Pie (savoury)

Sorry to be un-Australian for a moment, but I'm not talking about the individual meat pies that Aussies buy at a football game or a petrol station. If you're at the footy, you drink whatever beer you can get; it's not the time for food pairing and sniffing the beer in your plastic cup. And if you're grabbing a pie at a petrol station, it's probably not the time for a beer either.

But when you're eating a big, hearty pie with a rich filling – perhaps mince, steak and onion or a shepherd's pie – you want stout. A roasty stout that sits somewhere between 4% and 6% ABV is perfect for enjoying in a room full of dark timber and chattering people, preferably during winter. Take a bite of pie and a swig of stout and party like it's 1899.

Bonus points if the pie itself was cooked with stout in the gravy.

Chocolate brownie

Some would say to complement this with the chocolatey notes of a dark beer, but I reckon that just dulls the flavours of both beer and brownie, almost like they cancel each other out. What a waste of a good brownie and a good beer!

No, you want to contrast here – a raspberry sour will bring a slap of tartness to the sweet brownie, and is light enough that it won't weigh you down when paired with the decadent chocolate. You'll find the result is greater than the sum of its parts.

Of course, you could go for a different kind of sour – an orange sour would create a jaffa-like vibe, and cherry brings a wonderfully classy vibe to dark chocolate – but I'm a chocolate raspberry person.

Vanilla ice cream

Put a scoop into a glass of bitter chocolate stout. Thank me later.

section four

Here are my answers to some practical questions about beer. They're even more based in opinion and less based in research than the rest of the book, if that's possible.

Ask Mick

Q Does beer go bad?

It depends exactly what you're asking.

If you're asking if beer changes from its ideal flavour over time … yes, it does. Hoppy flavours are the first to be affected, so super hoppy beers that look to delicate hop oils for their intense flavours (such as hazy IPAs) are starting to shift in flavour after a few months. Most beers are still great for six to nine months. When you're pushing past this, a beer can still be good and enjoyable, but it won't taste the same as it did when it left the brewery. Some people will happily buy year-old beer, especially when it's discounted. Others won't bother spending their money here, and will pay a little more for the fresh stuff.

If you're asking if beer changes to a bad flavour over time … yes, it eventually does. How long it takes depends a bit on the beer and a lot on how the beer is treated.

If it's been kept out of the heat and light, the most likely thing to affect the smell and taste is the small amount of oxygen working on it over months and years. The beer will taste dull and stale, like wet cardboard. What a waste of a beer.

If a bottle of beer has been sitting in the sun, you'll smell sulphur when you open it. It'll taste like a skunk's spray. (Whether or not you've actually smelled a skunk … you don't want this for your beer.)

If it's become infected with (non-harmful) bacteria somewhere along the way, it'll taste sour, acidic or vinegary. If this wasn't supposed to be a sour beer, that'll ruin the flavour you were looking for when you picked up this beer. (Pasteurisation can protect against this.)

If you're asking if beer becomes unsafe to drink … no, it doesn't. Harmful bacteria can't thrive in beer – the brewing process includes sterilisation, and the alcohol and the hop acids are there to protect and serve. So never fear – you won't get food poisoning from bad beer.

But seriously – drink your beer as fresh as possible. It's better. *(See 'Fresh is Best' on page 125 for more information.)*

🄠 How do I introduce someone to beer?

First of all, don't force it on them. No one *has* to like beer. But if you have a friend who's willing to taste beers to see if they like them, here's what I'd do.

For many people who don't like beer, the main barrier is the bitterness from hops. So don't make the dumb move of giving them a west coast IPA straight up, no matter how much you love it. You want to find beers that are low in bitterness or have a strong balance of other tastes such as sweetness or sourness.

You can build up to bitterness. A hazy pale ale can surprise and please non-beer drinkers with its tropical fruit notes. Then, if someone likes this, they may want to eventually move up the bitterness scale, through punchier pale ales and easy-drinking juicy IPAs to all kinds of IPAs.

You can focus on malt. Someone with a sweet tooth may jump on the toffee and caramel notes of amber ales and red ales; these were a huge part of my introduction to flavoursome craft beer, and eventually I developed a taste for the hops hiding in them. If your friend likes some other intense flavours like coffee, dark chocolate, rum or whisky, try them with a dark beer. A smooth brown ale or chocolatey porter is a good place to start for most, but some people will take to stout like a duck to water. Me? I took a sip of a 14% ABV barrel-aged imperial stout and it blew my mind; I was hooked on dark beer from that day on. So don't be afraid to offer your friend some of the bigger brutes (particularly if they enjoy spirits).

You can look to the power of sour. For some of us, sourness brings its own obstacles to overcome, but others will light up at their first sip of a zingy sour. I particularly find that cider drinkers and wine drinkers often enjoy fruity sour beers right from the get-go. If you can find one, a Flanders red is a delightful place to begin ... but it's probably easier to find a local brewery that makes a raspberry or mango sour or something similar.

If someone <u>insists</u> that they don't like beer, you're not just trying to win over their tastebuds; you're trying to win over their mind.

They believe that they hate all beer (even though they've probably only tasted a narrow selection of beer flavours). Your goal is just to get them to say, 'Huh. I guess I don't hate *all* beer.' The way to do this is to offer them a beer that, in their mind, 'doesn't taste like beer'. Fruited sours can be good for this, but so can dessert beers. Try to find some crazy pastry stout – a double chocolate salted caramel stout or something like that – just to get them over their first hurdle.

And hey, sometimes the wild card pays off – I've seen non-beer drinkers won over by complex saisons, chewy double IPAs and smoked beers. We're all different.

Q How do I order a beer without sounding stupid?

It's easy to feel out of your depth at a beer bar. Maybe it's because you don't know what the beers are. There's a roggenbier or a faro on the list or some other style you're not familiar with? The beer name has the letters QDHSNEIIPA next to it or some other initials you don't recognise? Don't know what to expect from a San Diego pale ale or Vermont pale ale or Burton pale ale?

Sometimes it's because you don't know what the glass sizes are. I don't know how the beer world has stayed so bad at this. Some bars will helpfully list the volume amounts, but otherwise you can get lost easily. Schooner isn't a universal measurement for beer; the volume changes in different locations. An American pint is different to an imperial pint. And a bar may have 'small', 'medium' and 'large' glasses different to every other bar in the known universe. (At my favourite bar, the smallest size glass is called a bee's dick.)

My advice? Talk to the bartender. Honestly, just have a chat with them. They should be happy to help, and the more insider lingo involved (whether that's unusual beer styles or non-standard glass sizes or anything else), the more understanding they'll be that you're asking.

Be friendly and polite. This is good life advice for every situation, and how you should speak to any hospitality or retail worker … and here, it'll encourage the person you're talking with to be more helpful. Everyone prefers to deal with someone friendly and polite.

Ask questions. Don't complain that it isn't clear. Just ask. And if you change your mindset from 'I must get it right' to 'I want to find out more', both you and the server will have a better time. You don't need to feel stupid about not knowing. Just let your genuine curiosity guide the conversation, and you'll learn some cool things. And in heaps of breweries and independent bars, it's normal for the bartender to offer you a taste of a beer if you're not sure what to get.

Obviously if the bar is busy, you can't have a long conversation with the server. But they'll still help you out at busy times, and you can take the opportunity at quieter times to talk for longer and ask more questions.

You don't need a comprehensive guide, just an inquisitive mind.

ⓆＡre there any good non-alcoholic beers?

There are! Though this hasn't always been the case. There was a time when the only non-alc beers around tasted like water. Well, you know – very slightly beery water.

Actually, I take that back: non-alcoholic German beers have always been tasty. I suppose good beer is so important to German culture that German brewers have taken this endeavour seriously for a long time.

I visited Bali in the 2010s – a time when Australia was still sorely lacking in non-alcoholic beers – and was surprised at the number of alcohol-free beers in the stores.

Indonesia's large Muslim population has led to a strong market for non-alcoholic beers, so there's a range of them available there.

Many of the ones I saw were from big worldwide brands, but I'd never seen these alc-free options in Australia.

The rest of the world is catching up. There's been a generational shift in drinkers: in many countries, more people are health conscious than ever before, and more people are holding different views on alcohol, so there's a larger market for tasty low-alcohol and alcohol-free beer.

Brewers are fermenting beers with different yeast strains that don't produce alcohol like regular ale and lager yeast, and using different methods of removing alcohol from beer, and finding different ways of expressing flavour and making beer with body, so it's not all thin and weak and watery and boring.

As with everything, the larger breweries have more money to invest in research and technologies. But craft brewers put their innovation to good use, and in my mind, they're making the better tasting ones by a mile.

Q How do I acquire a taste for a beer style I don't like?

Acquired tastes are so interesting to me. It's not that you learn to tolerate a flavour you don't enjoy, but that you actually come to enjoy them – a lot. My favourite drinks are coffee, whisky and beer, and I started drinking all of them by persevering with them when I didn't enjoy the taste.

But I want to stress up front that there's no rule saying you *should* acquire a taste. It doesn't make you superior to enjoy certain foods or drinks. You could go the rest of your life drinking only sweet beers or only sour beers – or not drinking beer at all, of course – and you'd be fine.

But if you've decided you want to acquire a taste for certain beers, then here's some guidance. You've got to want it. You need a certain level of determination or intentionality. By definition, you're going to have to drink beers you don't like (yet), whether that's dark beers, sours, bitter IPAs or whatever else. But you can hold onto the fact that it's not just in your mind – your tastebuds literally change to accommodate what you eat and drink. Your determination will pay off.

You've got to stick with it. If you don't like sour beer, you probably won't acquire a taste for it after two or three. More likely you'll need to expose yourself to all kinds of different sour beers – easy-drinking Berliner weisses, salty goses, fruited kettle sours, sour IPAs, Flanders reds and browns, wild ales or even a lambic if you get your hands on one (though maybe share with a friend who likes lambic, so you're not wasting a rare or expensive beer!). As the taste of sourness itself becomes more familiar, you'll start to notice more and more nuances in these different kinds of beer. And even if you dislike every single sour you taste, you may find that you return to one a second or third time, maybe months later, and enjoy something you didn't enjoy before. I was shocked how much I enjoyed the juicy berry notes of a Flanders red after a few years of trying different sour beers.

You've got to enjoy the journey, in some sense. If you just sit at home hammering drinks you don't enjoy, you're not going to have a fun time. What a waste of a life.

But if you get together with some friends and share the beers and talk about them and pull a funny face with every sip, you're having a cool experience even if your tastebuds aren't on board. If you chat with a bartender or bottle shop server about what you do and don't enjoy, and ask for their recommendation on how you could move forward into new territory, you'll have an interesting conversation and probably learn a thing or two.

And you've got to be okay with the idea that this kind of flavour might not be for you. Don't get me wrong – it's almost certain that you'll dislike it less. But it may not become your new favourite. And that's fine. We're all different. That's why friends are interesting, beer is a never-ending journey and life is full of surprises.

Having said that … good luck!

Ⓠ How do I avoid becoming a beer snob?

We've all met our fair share of beer snobs. It's a sad fact that sometimes when a person is passionate about something, they look down on others who don't know as much as they do.

Thankfully, it's not inevitable. Learning to appreciate beer doesn't automatically make you into an insufferable jerk. You just have to watch that you don't pick up any bad habits, as tempting as they are.

Don't assume that you know more than other people.

Don't tell everyone everything you know about beer. Some people don't care and would rather talk about something else. And even most of the people who do care don't want a personal lecture.

Don't start name-dropping every brewer you've met or letting slip every rare beer you've tasted.

Don't judge people based on their beer choices. People can drink whatever they like.

Don't feel the need to correct every wrong thing that anyone ever says about beer.

Don't ignore your friends to spend ten minutes seducing the liquid in your cup, taking photos and writing notes. People come first.

Don't insult a small brewery on social media. If you don't like their beers, maybe complain to your friends in private and show your positive support for other breweries you do like, rather than damaging the reputation of a small business.

Do remember that people are more important than beer. If a friend pours your beer into the wrong glass, just say thank you instead of complaining. If someone at work buys you a 6-pack of a beer you wouldn't normally buy for yourself, just say thank you instead of crinkling your nose and passing it off to the closest person. If your father-in-law offers you a beer you'd never normally drink, accept it and enjoy it with him. Or if you really don't want it, say, 'No thanks,' and just drink something else without explaining to him that it's because that's actually not an independent beer and did you know they don't even lager their beer properly and in fact that beer is probably lightstruck because it's in a bottle and it's probably been sitting on a shelf in the heat so any hop character will have faded. Just say thanks.

Do be humble. When you gain a little knowledge on any topic, it's tempting to show off and try to impress people with a lot of facts at every opportunity. But it's much better to answer their questions with an appropriately brief level of detail (no lectures!) without making them feel stupid, and to let them know an interesting detail every now and then when it's relevant. People will be much more impressed – by your knowledge and by the fact that you're not scrambling for their approval or praise.

Do keep conversations about beer enjoyable and inclusive to the people around you. There's a time and a place for jargon-filled discussions with other beer lovers. But it may not be while others in the group are sitting there feeling stupid and left out, because they have nothing to contribute. And bitter arguments that show derision for certain brewers, breweries or other drinkers? No one wins these. Just give them a miss or back out of them graciously.

Do be serious about beer ... but don't take beer too seriously. It's supposed to be fun.

Q How do I become a brewer?

Don't come to me, that's for sure! My brain gets bored halfway through following a recipe for making choc chip cookies and I end up changing half the ingredients, setting the oven at a random temperature and forgetting to set a timer. No one wants me to be the person in charge of making sure the tanks have been properly sterilised or that wort has the right levels of fermentable sugars. I'd probably change the variety, amount and timing of the hops at the last minute 'just to see what happens ...'

But here's what I'd say you could do ...

Learn as much about beer as you can. (See next question.)

Take up home brewing and join home brewing groups.

Talk to brewers. Ask them questions about brewing. Ask them for advice on how to become a brewer. Ask them for a job! I know plenty of brewers who started out working for a brewery in a different role and ended up getting the chance to move into the brewing part of the business – even though they had no previous brewing experience.

Get some formal brewing training. There are certificates and degrees available at various institutions. Some have to be attended entirely in person, while others have a large component that can be done remotely. These qualifications aren't always necessary to work in brewing, but they're well recognised.

Q Where do I go from here?

Get to know other beer lovers. Make friends with punters at your favourite bars and breweries. Introduce yourself to the staff. Go to events and masterclasses and beer festivals. Join online communities and chat on forums – home brewer groups and forums are particularly collaborative.

Where possible, talk to the people who make and sell beer. Drink at your local brewery and ask questions about beer styles and the brewing process, and find out the story of this brewer and this brewery itself. See the passion in the eyes of people who see beer as more than just a product. Getting excited about beer is just as important as learning more information.

Chase down more knowledge. The casual approach is to read articles on the internet and buy books about beer. The discerning learner might be interested in the BJCP Style Guidelines *(see 'Beer styles' on page 63)*, which are available to download from the BJCP website as a free PDF and contain a wealth of information. If you want to learn in a more structured way, the Cicerone Certification Program has online courses that teach anyone more about beer or you could study and take the exams to become a Cicerone – a certified beer expert.

Find new beer experiences. Book a brewery tour. Visit Germany, Belgium, England or different regions of the States to see what the beer culture is like.

Make your own beer experiences. Organise a brewery crawl. Get a tasting flight of four beers and see if you can describe the differences in flavour. Invite friends over to compare five different IPAs or perhaps to try five new styles of beer you haven't tasted before. Start a beer journal and reflect on the beers you drink: jot down notes about appearance, aroma, taste, mouthfeel and any other thoughts or associations.

Most importantly: have fun. You don't always have to be switched on when you're drinking beer. Sometimes it pays to just lean back and enjoy a fresh beer as a way to unwind, to let beer be the liquid backdrop while you're catching up with a friend.

Beer is meant to be enjoyed. Don't let anyone take that away from you.

Acknowledgements

Writing can be a solitary activity. But this book is a team achievement, and I'd like to thank these players …

James Smith of The Crafty Pint – for his support, constant encouragement and friendship. He's also been paying me to write about beer for years, which has grown my beer knowledge and honed my writing skills. Without him, this book wouldn't exist.

The team at Rockpool Publishing. They took my words and turned them into a book, and made the process easy for me. Special mention to Daniel and Ellie for the aesthetic awesomeness, and to Luke for championing me the whole way.

My friend Daniel who let me pick his brains for all those little details about brewing that I was unsure of.

My 'cousin-in-law' Andre for offering to be the first to read over my work in progress.

My friends Will and Judd, who lent me their eyes as fellow beer writers to make sure I hadn't said anything (too) stupid.

All the brewers who have taught me about beer and talked me through the brewing process over the years. They're the real beer experts. I'm just the middle man.

My darling wife Kamina. She patiently tolerates me taking notes about beers, and disappearing to write, and taking over the fridge with beers. But more than this, she uses her big brain to help me, and her bigger heart to support and encourage me always. She keeps me grounded and she lifts me up. She's the best.

About the author

Mick Wüst has been writing about beer since 2015.
He works for the The Crafty Pint, an Australian craft beer website,
writing articles that are fun and informative (in that order). He's also
a freelance writer for other beer businesses and publications.

Mick's worked as a pastor, a lecturer and a barista, and he runs
regularly to keep the beer belly at bay. He lives in Brisbane (the best
city) with his wife (the best person). This is his first book.